The Young Mastermind

*Become the Master of
Your Own Mind*

Muhammad Ali

The Young Mastemind

Become the Master of Your Own Mind

© 2018 Muhammad Ali

All rights reserved. No part of this book may be reproduced, stored in a retrieval system, or transmitted, in any form or by any means, electronic, mechanical, photocopying, recording, scanning, or otherwise - except for brief quotations in critical reviews or articles, without the prior written permission of the publisher.

Printed in the Kingdom of Saudi Arabia. Published in Toronto, Canada, by Mastermind Publishing House.

ISBN: 978-1-7752569-1-5 (Paperback)

ISBN: 978-1-7752569-0-8 (eBook)

Copyright © 2016 by Young Masterminds Institute of Success

This book is dedicated to every single human being in this Universe including YOU.

Connect with Muhammad Ali on social media:

Instagram.com/Young.Mastermind

YouTube.com/YoungMastermind

Facebook.com/MasterAliMind

Twitter.com/MasterAliMind

Contents

Author's Preface vii

Chapter 1 *Introduction* 9

Chapter 2 *Secretum Secretorum* 15

Chapter 3 *The 360° Flip* 29

Chapter 4 *6ix Minutes to Success* 39

Chapter 5 *Thinking to Grow Rich..?* 51

Chapter 6 *Do What Successful People Do* 65

Chapter 7 *The Mirror to Success* 93

Chapter 8 *Education as Entertainment* 109

Chapter 9 *Serene Thinking* 133

Chapter 10 *Money 101* 155

Chapter 11 *Futile Fear* 173

Chapter 12 *Master the Present* 187

Acknowledgements 199

Author's Preface

My name is Muhammad Ali, and at the age of 19, I came into a state of *Conscious Awareness* after I crossed paths with an initiate of an ancient fraternity. This fraternity traces its knowledge through the golden age of Arab civilization back centuries to ancient Egypt and Sumeria. It prides itself on including many of the wealthiest men in history, some of whom founded great empires, magnificent cities, and spectacular structures. The initiate I met, named Ahmed, asked me to spend sometime with him. When I did, he provided me with valuable information that bridged my new knowledge with its ancient middle eastern origins. He then requested me to serve humanity by sharing my journey of mental transformation with others in the form of a book. I met him at a waterfront location where I found myself answering specific detailed questions about my journey, which resulted in the compilation of the contents of this book in just five hours.

My purpose for writing this book is to bring people on the path that would lead them to reach the ideal state of *Conscious Awareness*. This book will show YOU how to become the **Master of your own Mind!**

While reading this book, you will come across unique insights that will alter your perspective on life in a positive way. IF you read this book more than once and practically follow every **M**aster

Action **P**lan at the end of each chapter, then I guarantee you will transform your thinking to that of a *Mastermind*. If you are seeking higher truths to life, then you will notice the golden bars of ancient wisdom and superior knowledge that emit light and diminish darkness. This book contains information that illustrates how to stay in a Mastermind vibrational frequency as opposed to the frequency of a Sleepwalker. I invite you to read my story on how I transformed from a *Sleepwalker* into a being a *Young Mastermind*.

Chapter 1

Introduction

Who is Muhammad Ali and
why you should read his book?

It all started when a young Scottish lady by the name of Ella Allen at the age of 16 dreamt of a cube at the center of planet earth. Ella Allen's uncle was a very close friend and business associate of Andrew Carnegie. Mr. Carnegie grew to become known as the wealthiest men alive in his era. A year later she could not forget her magnificent dream, and she later discovered that the cube she saw was the Holy Kaaba in the city of Mecca. Ella woke up into a state of *Conscious Awareness* with a burning desire to visit this holy place in the Kingdom of Saudi Arabia. The dream remained with her and led her to meet a young nobleman of established Arabian ancestral roots who was a foreign student at the University of Edinburgh. She shared her dream with him and became fond of him as he was a practicing Mastermind. They both planned on getting married after she turned 18 and a year later, Ella embraced Islam with the intention to fulfill her worthy ideal and reach her desired destination; the Holy Kaaba.

The married couple had two boys in Scotland. The eldest son

dedicated his life to working for the United Nations at the International Atomic Energy Agency in Vienna. The younger son joined the British army, became a Lt. Colonel and was later appointed as the official Military Secretary for the last Nizam of Hyderabad. The ancient city, Hyderabad became a favorite destination for Arab soldiers under the Asaf Jahi dynasty, popularly known as the Nizams. In 1849, there were around 5,000 Arabs in the Nizam's army. The last Nizam was featured on the cover of Time Magazine as the *"Richest Man In The World"* and described by Forbes as the 5th all-time wealthiest human being in history. In the year 1955, His Majesty King Saud bin Abdulaziz Al Saud came to visit the H.E.H the Nizam of Hyderabad. In gratitude for the King's official visit, a year later the Nizam dispatched an official delegation led by his Military Secretary; my maternal great-grandfather, to the two holy cities, Mecca and Medina. My great grandfather invited his parents, including his mother, Ella who took on the Arabic name *Halima* and accompanied him to perform the Hajj at the center of planet earth. That great dream she once had to behold the sacred Kaaba, became her reality. Her faith and persistence in relentlessly holding this goal on the screen of her mind with certainty, patience, and serenity ended up manifesting into physical form. I learned of this side of my family's remarkable history when I found an old photograph of my great-grandfather with King Saud on the official website of the King Saud Foundation.

In 1995, well after my great-grandfather was retired, he met a graduate from Caltech. This man served my great-grandfather for years as his admiration for this young man grew to such an extent that he introduced him to his granddaughter. These two human beings ended up getting married, and ***The Young Mastermind*** was born on planet earth. I, Muhammad Ali, give my deepest gratitude to Ella Allen, because of her decision to pursue her dream, I am blessed to be alive and able to live in the prosperous Kingdom with my parents. Since Ella Allen's dream came true for her, I was inspired to pursue the publishing of this book!

I'm nineteen years old, and I was born in Canada. When I was seven, my family and I moved back to Saudi Arabia due to my dad's new occupation as a senior project manager for a multinational corporation. I went to a private school ranked amongst the top three in the Kingdom. The campus size of this school was as large as a university campus! My classmates included Al-Saud royalty and other super-rich families of the Kingdom. I saw kids come to school daily in Rolls Royces, Bentleys, Maybachs, Lamborghinis, Porches, Ferraris, and Aston Martins. I knew students whose families were so rich that members of their immediate family would travel in private jets to Paris just for a haircut! From a young age, my life was populated by people who came from the wealthiest Arab families in the world. This environmental exposure programmed my mind to *desire* a rich life. In my perception 'success' meant living an opulent life with an abundance of material objects.

My mom, a spiritual life coach who traces her roots to Arabian nobles (Shurafa), emphasized reading from a very young age. Our home library included classics from both Western and Eastern traditions that intended to facilitate my intellectual growth. As I grew older, I rarely read any books until the day I found a few book series that entertained me. I believe that school played a role in dampening my love for reading because of the mandatory readings which didn't entertain me. At the age of 13, I came across a book series, Captain Underpants by Dav Pilkey that caught my attention, and after that, I started reading Diary of a Wimpy Kid by Jeff Kinney. Given my age, I related to these books and found them easy to read. I finished reading these books before the tenth grade and abruptly stopped reading for no clear reason. I reached a point where I didn't read required stories for English class and watched the movie instead.

At this stage in my life, my mom introduced me to a famous movie, *The Secret*, and she gave me a copy of *The Secret to Teen Power* by Paul Harrington for my 15th birthday. After reading the book, I started to become aware of an ancient science that suggested I could use the power of my own mind to attract anything I want into my life. This universal scientific idea called the Law of Attraction (*Haqiqat al-Jadhbah*) was transmitted through the ancient writings of Jabir ibn Hayyan (Geber) who was a disciple of the Alchemist Ja'far al- Sadiq. Furthermore, ibn Hayyan translated the Emerald Tablet into Arabic as, *The Book of the Secret of Creation and the Art of Nature* (**Kitab sirr al-Khaliqa**). This is the earliest dated source and translation of the Hermetica and the Law of Attraction.

I began to experiment with what I was learning to improve my life positively so every year I would attract the opportunity to explore different countries around the world. Growing up I had the luxury of visiting the Great Pyramids of Giza in Egypt, Petra in Jordan, Blue Mosque in Turkey, Burj Khalifa in the United Arab Emirates, Taj Mahal in India, Niagara Falls in Canada, Big Ben in the United Kingdom, Marina Bay in Singapore, Twin Towers in Malaysia, and the most visited site on earth, the Holy Kaaba in Mecca, Saudi Arabia. Traveling expanded my perception of life by making me realize the abundance of opulence there is in nature as that's where genuine success resides. Wherever I traveled in the world, my attention would be focused on luxuries, such as mansions, exotic vehicles, yachts, and private jets. The lavish lifestyle of the young Saudi royals and multi-billionaires allowed me to BELIEVE that desert money wasn't a mirage after all. This mindset got me to consciously accept that being super rich is attainable.

However, given I was very new to understand the Law of Attraction, the greatest challenge I faced was that I didn't have the proper guidance in place to teach and remind me how to utilize my mind to gradually bridge the gap between this burning desire and my reality.

My desire to find a golden key that would unlock the master key to infinite riches led me on a mental journey in search for what has been referred to as the *Strangest Secret to Success...*

Chapter 2

Secretum Secretorum

"This is the truth, the whole truth and nothing but the truth: - as below, so above; as above so below. With this knowledge alone you may work miracles"

-Jabir ibn Hayyan

Did you know that YOU were born rich? If it's hard for you to believe that, then you will soon realize this truth about yourself. From as far back as I can remember I have always had the inner desire to be rich. As a 19 year old, I understand that I always desired a life of comfort and freedom, which is why I desired riches. Richness doesn't only mean material wealth; it also means a life of abundance. Many successful individuals from history mention that human beings were born rich. If you are a human being, just remember that you were actually born rich, because humans are the highest forms of creation and you have been blessed with the ability to THINK. Understand the act of *thinking* is the most powerful function that you can do as a human being! I'm not sure if you are aware of this fact, but there is an actual goldmine between both of your ears. It is called the MIND! So basically...YOU were born with the most powerful asset in the entire universe; your mind.

If you desire to live a happy, healthy and wealthy life, then you naturally want to master the game of life. In order to do this successfully, you need to learn how to become the master of your own mind. The world's most successful people from history and the 21st Century only became 'successful' after they developed a burning desire! Desire represents the natural urge of life that wants to express more of itself through you. If you want ANYTHING in life, then understand that you can have it only if you desire it. At times you may feel like what you desire is too good to be true, but always remember your mind is only able to *think* of a desire because it is possible for you to attain that desire. Your mind cannot be conscious of a desire unless the possibility of its fulfillment exists. This means that as long as you have a desire to be, do, or have something, then it is 100% realistic for you to actually manifest your desire!

"Mind is the Master power

that molds and makes.."

-James Allen

Once I developed the burning **desire** to be rich and live a successful life, regardless of any circumstance, I couldn't give up on what I wanted. I always imagined I would be very rich one day, but I never had an awareness of how to accomplish that goal. Throughout my childhood, popular tv shows and movies programmed to my mind to believe that high schools' in North America were the 'coolest' places on earth to study at with freedom. This influenced me to such an extent that I thought if I were to study at a Canadian high school, I would be able to experience that 'successful' lifestyle. As the years went by, my mind was manifesting this dream without me even realizing and it soon became my reality!

I would spend every summer in Toronto with family, but in the summer of 2014, after my vacation was over, I ended up staying longer than I expected due to some unforeseen events. This meant, for the time being, I had to forget about returning to my private high school in the Kingdom and instead attend a public school in Canada. This was the point in my life where I experienced a crazy culture shock! I started the tenth grade at a high school but during my time at this school, my 'popularity' grew by the day, and I began making a lot of friends with different types of people. Some of these friends were very distracting because they were predominantly occupied with a lifestyle significantly different from what I had been used to in the Kingdom. Over the course of those months, I developed various associations that had both positive and negative impacts on me. The next part of my story requires you to understand an advanced way of thinking, so I will further elaborate what I mean. Albert Einstein once said, *"Concerning matter, we have been all wrong. What we have called matter is energy, whose vibration has been so lowered as to be perceptible to the senses. There is no matter."*

According to the Law of Vibration, every single thing in this universe is *energy*, which vibrates at a particular frequency. People with positive energy vibrate at higher frequencies while people with negative energy vibrate at lower frequencies. In grade ten, I never knew how this universe operates with energy so I allowed my mind to easily get influenced by people with negative energy because I was programmed by the media to think that people who do wrong things are considered 'successful'. My ***desire*** was to be 'successful' so whatever my mind believed, my body acted upon and that lead me to attract either positive or negative results in my life. As I continued to hang out with the 'cool kids', my own positive energy started becoming negative. Bad habits became automatic as I continued to remain unaware. Focusing on education at that point in my life was one of my lowest priorities. I was heading down the opposite path of success at a very young age, but at that point, I thought that it was the path of 'success'. I started to notice the more I associated with people who had bad habits, the more popular I became. I may have looked happy on the outside, but internally I was a mess. At that point in my life, I was able to recall my middle school math teacher's advice. Mr. Williams was the type of teacher who entertained the class with stories that had valuable life lessons. Till this very day, I can still hear what he once said, "Whichever type of people you surround yourself with, you will end up becoming like those people." Even though deep down I knew he was right, I continued to hang out with the 'bad kids' between classes and after school because I would *feel* like the center of attention. Things started to get from bad to worse, as I attracted, even more, negative circumstances into my life each day. I would come home late from school because I would waste my time doing stupid things with different people. I would stay up all night to text my 'friends' and then fall asleep in math class the following morning. My grades were a complete disaster and I was proud at the same time! At this point in my life, I was at ground zero mainly because I was living for my egotistical desires rather than living for my purpose.

One afternoon I received an unexpected phone call from my dad with some news. He told me that my flight back to Jeddah was in a couple of hours and I needed to pack my bags ASAP! The moment I heard that I was really disappointed because I wanted to say goodbye to all my friends in person but there wasn't even enough time. However, I was able to successfully return to my private high school in the Kingdom and reconnect with my old friends. When I got back, I had to readjust myself to the environment, as I felt the burden of catching up on everything that was going on and work extra hard to re-establish my so-called 'popularity' at school.

Fast forward two years later, I successfully graduated from high school. Today I am back in Toronto at a new condo near campus and a week away from starting the program of my choice at a university that accepted me on a scholarship. After settling in, I was planning on getting in touch with some of my old friends from tenth grade, but for some strange reason, regardless of how hard we tried to connect, my friends and I were unable to meet physically in person. When I told my mentor about this issue, I learned it was nothing other than the fact that my old friends and I no longer vibrated on the same frequency. In an attempt to better understand what he meant, I carefully analyzed all changes in my thinking, behavior, and associations after I left Canada in the tenth grade to where I am today in my life. I have consciously realized that I used to be a Sleepwalker...

The 12 characteristics of **Sleepwalkers**:

Sleepwalkers are human beings that are ungrateful.

Sleepwalkers are human beings that cannot articulate exactly what they really WANT in life.

Sleepwalkers are human beings that don't know why they are doing the things they do in their everyday lives.

Sleepwalkers are human beings that are unaware of their *Infinite Potential* that is seeking expression from within.

Sleepwalkers are human beings that don't THINK for themselves; rather they follow the masses.

Sleepwalkers are human beings that continue to allow negative forms of entertainment to program their minds, even after being aware of the harmful effects.

Sleepwalkers are human beings that are content with mediocre habits.

Sleepwalkers are human beings that tiptoe through life in fear.

Sleepwalkers are human beings that resist lifelong learning.

Sleepwalkers are human beings that *love* money and *use* people.

Sleepwalkers are human beings that choose to *React* instead of *Respond*.

Sleepwalkers are human beings that are unaware of the gift they have in every moment of their lives.

Sleepwalkers are human beings that don't *desire* growth.

The Law of Polarity states that every single thing has an opposite to it. The exact opposite of a Sleepwalker is a Mastermind. Sleepwalkers live in darkness while Masterminds live in the light.

In the Arabic language, sleepwalkers are referred to as people who live in a state of ***Ghafla***

If at this moment, you feel like you might be a Sleepwalker, understand that you are blessed, because there are Sleepwalkers in every single city on planet earth that don't even realize they are sleepwalking. If you don't feel like you are a sleepwalker then understand that you are also blessed, because you are now on the journey to becoming the **MASTER OF YOUR OWN MIND!**

In the last month, right before I graduated from my high school in the Kingdom, I made the committed decision to never be a sleepwalker who tiptoes through life in fear hoping to make it safely to the grave. After I took action and consciously made that Master Decision, my whole life started to change in such a positive way and it kept on getting better by the day!

Master Action Plan

1) Do you enjoy reading? If the answer is "NO", then ask yourself why is it that you dislike the act of reading. Who or what caused you to dislike reading?

2) Do you want to be rich in all areas of your life?

If the answer is "not really", then ask yourself why not.

Who or what caused you to feel uncomfortable to think or talk about money and riches?

3) Define what the word 'freedom' means to you.

Who or what caused you to feel uncomfortable to think or talk about money?

4) Why don't you want to be a Sleepwalker?

5) Remember people with positive energy vibrate on higher frequencies while people with negative energy vibrate on lower frequencies. Which type of people do you want to associate with?

Name 5 people in your life who give off negative energy:

1)

2)

3)

4)

5)

Name 5 people in your life who give off positive energy:

1)

2)

3)

4)

5)

If you desire to always give off positive energy then stop surrounding yourself with the first 5 people!

Chapter 3

The 360° Flip

"I'd rather welcome change
than cling to the past"

-Robert Kiyosaki

Throughout my childhood, Tony Hawk was my role model as I loved skateboarding. I did not get influenced to get tattoos, but I definitely got influenced to take risks in life! I wanted to learn how to do a 360-degree flip like a professional skater. Tony Hawk was known to be the only skater at that time who successfully accomplished a 360-degree loop stunt. I eventually got to do a 360, and I will never forget the day this happened, but it wasn't with a skateboard, it was with my life!

My dad's birthday was coming up, so my mom and I went to a local Virgin Megastore in Jeddah to pick out a book as a birthday gift for him. As I was in exploring the business section, a book with a purple cover immediately grabbed my attention. The book was *Rich Dad Poor Dad For Teens* by Robert Kiyosaki. I was drawn to the subtitle, **_"The Secrets About Money - That You Don't Learn In School!"_** While I was used to spending hundreds of dollars on video games, I hesitated to invest in myself at that very moment and purchase the book, although it only costs a fraction of what my video games did. In retrospect, I am my most valuable asset, and I always invest in myself because that is the most valuable investment I can make.

I thought that if the subtitle by itself confirmed my inner belief about money and school, the contents of the book would have incredible insights in store for me. Later that week the book crossed my mind again, but this time I acted upon the thought and immediately got the eBook. I started reading the book on my phone, and the first chapter alone was so intriguing that I couldn't stop until I completed it. I took advantage of every opportunity to read the book: on the way to school, in the car with my parents, in classes when there was nothing to do, and in situations where I was waiting for something or someone. I was hooked on the author's story and his teachings, but this book was incomparable to the previous books I chose to read. Eventually, I introduced *Rich Dad Poor Dad* to my high school best friend, and he loved it as well. We used to talk about it often, and sometimes we made inside jokes in class like, *"you are all stuck in the rat race!"* This became our mantra for months. The most important lesson I learned from this book is the author's explanation of the mediocre lifestyle. Below is a summary of Robert Kiyosaki's explanation of the **Rat Race.**

If you look at the life of the average-educated, hard-working person, there is a similar path. The child is born and goes to school. The proud parents are excited because the child excels, gets fair to good grades, and is accepted into a college. The child graduates from school and maybe goes on to graduate school and then does exactly as programmed: searches for a safe, secure job or career. The child finds that job, maybe as a doctor or a lawyer, or an engineer, or an accountant, or joins the Army or works for the government. Generally, the child begins to make money, credit cards start to arrive in mass, and the shopping begins, if it already hasn't. Having money to burn, the child goes to places where other young people just like them hang out, and they meet people, they date, and sometimes they get married. Life is wonderful now, because today, both men and women work. Two incomes are bliss. They feel successful, their future is bright, and they decide to buy a house, a car, television, take vacations and have children. The happy bundle arrives. The demand for cash is enormous! The happy couple decides that their careers are vitally important and begin to work harder, seeking promotions and raises. The raises come, and so does another child and the need for a bigger house. They work harder, become better employees, that are even more dedicated. They go back to school to get more specialized skills so they can earn more money. Maybe they take a second job. Their incomes go up, but so does the tax bracket they're in and the real estate taxes on their new large home, and their Social Security taxes, and all the other taxes. They get their large paycheck and wonder where all the money went. They buy some mutual funds and buy groceries with their credit card. The children reach 5 or 6 years of age, and the need to save for college increases as well as the need to save for their retirement.

That 'happy' couple, born 35 years ago, is now trapped in the Rat Race for the rest of their working days. They work for the owners of their company, for the government paying taxes, and for the bank paying off a mortgage and credit cards. Then, they advise their own children to *'study hard, get good grades, and find a safe job or career.'* They learn nothing about money, except those who profit from their naivetés and work hard all the years of their lives. The process repeats itself into another hard-working generation. This is the **Rat Race'**.

Do you want to join this royal race for rats?

My best friend was so captivated by the book that he finished reading every chapter before I did. This book teaches the fundamentals of how to attain money in the real world, emphasizes the importance of financial education, and delivers practical success strategies for young minds. Robert Kiyosaki made me realize that most forms of traditional education do not provide the in-depth knowledge that is practical for attaining riches. It fails to train students how to reach the state of financial freedom and live life on their own terms. I needed the financial education to learn how to reach the state of financial freedom, yet I found myself in high school learning trigonometry, balancing chemical equations, and reading Shakespeare. While classes like these gave me good information, they did not satisfy my needs for what I was seeking to learn.

After reading *Rich Dad Poor Dad*, I became aware that the educational path I was on, was setting me up for the Rat Race. My education was not equipping me for financial freedom. This was when I reached a major crossroad in my life. I was totally confused and saw no roads to success. I did not look forward to spending the rest of my life as an employee working for money. I wanted to reverse the equation by becoming an entrepreneur and learn how to make money work for me. I could never imagine myself working for an employer who is on top of the corporate pyramid and remain enslaved to a system that would only grant me 'freedom' when I became too old and sick to enjoy life. At this point, I really needed the self-confidence to be persistent in pursuing my desire to be financially free. Thankfully, my uncle introduced my mom to the concept of mentorship when I was small as that exposure allowed me to believe that if I were to learn from someone who had what I wanted in life, then I would be able to follow their footsteps to success and avoid all the common mistakes along the way. Mentorship is the idea of learning from someone who has already achieved the things you desire to achieve in life.

The quest for a mentor led me to find a, young, charismatic, dominant life coach from California known as *'JC'* who began to motivate me to the extent that I started taking ACTION on improving my life. As a highly energetic guy, he inspired me to take the role of a *player* in life rather than be a typical *spectator*. He instilled his fascination with books in me, which in turn got me to think that reading a book was actually 'cool'. I was amazed at how someone so unique could also be so passionate about reading. His aggressive rejection to settle for an average life captivated me, as I made the committed decision to never to be a part of mediocrity and conform to other people's standards without *thinking* for myself.

"Men simply don't think!"

-Dr. Albert Schweitzer

I had reached the point in life where I knew that if I didn't get out of my comfort zone and dream to live an extraordinary life that's full of genuine happiness, life-long health and an abundance of wealth, then I would continue to be a *sleepwalker*. It was time for me to fully transform myself into a *Mastermind* who dominates his path to success! I didn't have connections or resources but I did have a burning *desire* to gain the wisdom that would expand my level of awareness so I could learn how to become the Master of my own Mind.

Master Action Plan

1) Does the idea of living a life trapped in the 'Rat Race' scare you?

2) Why do you want to avoid getting trapped in the Rat Race?

3) Do you feel like you are already trapped in the daily cycle of 'life'? If you answer "Yes", then are you confident enough to break the Master Lock of Life, so you can successfully escape the Rat Race? If you feel like you are confident enough, then I suggest you get out of your comfort zone to break the pattern and do something different!

The 360° Flip

Chapter 4

6ix Minutes to Success

"Success is the progressive realization

of a worthy ideal"

-Earl Nightingale

On the night of March 7th in the year 2016, I was scrolling through some beneficial videos on YouTube, and suddenly my beautiful eyes spotted a video titled, **"All You Need is Six Minutes Each Day To Success"**. The first reason I just called my eyes 'beautiful' is because I am extremely grateful to my eyes for spotting that video as if it weren't them, I would still be Sleepwalking. The second reason is that I love myself, as every human should. All truly happy people practice self- love. If you want to live with genuine happiness, start practicing self-love. Anyways, before I get off subject let me continue with this phenomenal life changing story!

The title of that video piqued my interest, and within seconds I found myself watching it keenly. A dignified elderly man dressed in a sharp suit, standing inside a beautiful wooden office introduced himself as 'Bob Proctor'. His natural charisma captivated me. He spoke with a deep wisdom that held my attention. Bob talked about traveling all around the world helping people understand the real secrets to success. In the video, he briefly shared components of his life story and the steps he had taken to become successful. He began with sharing the secret that really changed his life. Mr. Bob Proctor is the Chairman and Co-Founder of the Proctor Gallagher Institute that operates all over the world. With over fifty-seven years of experience, authority, and proven results, he is considered the world's foremost expert on the human mind and leader in the personal development industry. You may recognize him through the award-winning film, *The Secret*. He has appeared on a variety of television channels, published in major publications, and has helped millions of people understand themselves and their minds.

As I paid attention, Bob explained how his life hadn't always been so successful. At the age of twenty-six, he had been an average guy who worked at a fire station in Toronto. As soon as I heard that, I started smiling because I was born there. In the video, Bob said that back then he earned $4,000 a year, but owed people $6,000. According to Bob, in 1961, people considered that a significant amount of money. He was satisfied with the average results he was getting in life, and he never thought of changing direction. Even when he had considered a change, he hadn't been aware of how to accomplish it. This was when Ray Stanford; Bob's friend introduced Bob to the classic book *Think and Grow Rich* by Napoleon Hill. Ray Stanford was a happy, healthy, wealthy man and Bob looked up to him. Ray advised him to follow the instructions of the book if he wanted to be happy, healthy, and wealthy. Bob knew how to read, but he had never been interested in reading. For some strange reason, however, he started reading the book, just like the way you are reading this book. Napoleon Hill said that his book contains a secret, and if you find that secret, you can have anything you really want in life. Bob Proctor received mentorship from the western founder of the personal development industry; Earl Nightingale. He had such a deep understanding of the subject of human achievement. Earl's exact definition of success is very simple but profound as well. *"Success is the progressive realization of a worthy ideal."* If you have decided that you are willing to dedicate your time to accomplish a specific goal, and you are constantly aware that you're moving in the direction towards achieving that goal on a daily basis, then you are automatically considered 'successful' according to Earl Nightingale. After Bob applied what he learned, his entire life changed dramatically over a short period of time that he started earning millions of dollars despite the fact that he went to high school for only two months!

I instantly recognized Bob's story as the inspiration I needed to start my journey as it revamped my *desire* for riches. I subscribed to his email list and received more videos right away. He also talked about how all people are programmed to think and do things in a certain way. I found the concepts he discussed very interesting, and I desired to grasp a deeper understanding of his teachings. I had no idea where this would take me, and before I even knew it, I attracted unlimited access to Bob's audio programs. I made sure I downloaded them onto my phone the night before school. Every morning on the way to school, I would listen to his audio recordings, which led me to become aware of the fact that my mind has the power to do EVERYTHING I want it to do and attract ANYTHING I desire into my life. After diving even more deeply into this golden wisdom, I was mesmerized by what I was learning and I kept on feeling extremely grateful because I couldn't imagine living my life without the awareness that I developed. I then started to realize that majority of people on this planet aren't even aware of their *Infinite Potential* that is locked up but is seeking expression from within. Miraculously finding Bob Proctor when I was 18 felt like I found the last piece to life's success puzzle that most people never find! One lesson led to another insight and my life started changing in such a positive way that I would need an actual telescope to look back to where I was in life to where I am now. The superior knowledge that I was seeking to learn became mine and I started gaining ancient wisdom from one mentor to another as I was guided. My level of awareness kept on expanding to such an extent that adults started asking me to mentor them, even though I was only 19. It got to a point that a lady from California offered me $10,000 to coach her. After I graduated from high school I wrote down a goal that sacred and excited me at the exact same time; to meet Bob Proctor in person and learn from him. I never let a doubtful thought enter my mind and I just had a pure belief that this dream would somehow manifest. I didn't focus on 'HOW' it was going to happen because I just had the faith that it was bound to happen. Things started to manifest before my very eyes and one person led to another and before I knew it, I was in sitting in his office!

The first time I got the opportunity to meet Bob Proctor in person was on November 8, 2016, at the Sheraton Hotel in Toronto, Canada. I am forever grateful to his wife Linda because she opened the doors to the seminar room for me before the event started. I can still see the crystal clear image of this scene taking place in my imagination. As my head turned over my right shoulder, I see Bob standing twelve feet away from me. At first, I hesitated to make a decision on what I should do, but then I followed my intuition and took ACTION as I started walking toward him to introduce myself in a respectable manner. I looked him in the eyes and said aloud, *"I AM so happy and grateful that I'm able to be in this moment right now."* I started the conversation in the **M**aster **A**ttitude of **G**ratitude. I then told him about my Master Mission in life and the valuable service to which I have dedicated my life to render. In that conversation, I told Bob that the superior knowledge and information that he shares in a unique way must be taught to the younger generation of Saudi Arabia and the rest of the world. I explained to him how I am only going to focus on empowering youth. He looked at me piercingly and said,

> *"Forget about age, age is irrelevant. There is no such thing as age in space, there is no time in space. Age is an illusion. The mind of a ten-year- old works the same as the mind of a ninety-year- old. The only difference in a little kid is they lack vocabulary and experience, other than that you can talk to a little kid the same way as you talk to an adult. Their mind is the same mind, there is only 1 mind."*

Do YOU want to be young forever? I'm guessing you would if you could. Most people never imagine being young forever, but some people do because they choose to believe in the 'impossible'. After Bob had waked me up to this higher level of awareness, I realized that he was right. Age is really just an illusion. We have been programmed to believe that when a person gets old, great experiences in life fade away; that being tired, sick, and even poor, is what an old person must experience. Whoever accepts this idea will end up attracting these things into their life as they get older. Regardless of how crazy this may sound, I genuinely believe that YOU can be 'young' for as long as you desire. Understand that idea of being 'young' doesn't mean physically although that is a by-product, it means adopting a *young* mindset.

Always remember, your conscious mind has the power to either accept or reject any idea, so use this power to disregard all the false ideas that society induces and choose to believe that you will never get old. If you act like you are going to be young forever and make your mind think, feel and behave every day as if you were always going to be young then I guarantee you are going to be young for as long as you want. Bob Proctor is a living proof that adopting this way of *thinking* actually works! Bob rejected all the conventional ideas of being 'old' a long time ago, and that is why he is eighty-three years old but looks much younger and has more energy than people half his age.

I titled this book *'The Young Mastermind'* because I feel like billions of human beings all around the globe would love to think, feel, and act young, rather than old. So that is why reading this book and joining me on this journey will not only help you become the Master of Your Own Mind but transform you into a *Young Mastermind!*

Master Action Plan

1) Is there someone in your life that you admire, perceive as successful or aspire to be like? This person could even be someone from history.

Once you decide who that person is and you have a desire to be as successful as them, then just follow their footsteps and do what they did, and you are bound to get what they got. However, you must study them and learn what they did so you can get to where they got in life.

2) You may recall this from one of my programs called *Mastering the Art of Self-Love*. Whenever you look in the mirror, what do you notice yourself thinking or saying about the image in the reflection? If you find yourself thinking about all the parts of your face, body or hair that you dislike then you can never be truly happy.

If you want to experience genuine happiness, then you must shift your attention, focus on all the things that you like about that image in the mirror and *feel* grateful.

3) Do you really believe that YOU actually have *Infinite Potential*?

If you doubt what I just stated, don't worry because you will soon gain an understanding about the infinite power that your MIND has and once you genuinely believe that, then there is not a single thing you won't be able to do in this life!

4) Do you believe in the idea that the older you get; the slower life gets? If you do, then I want you to reject that idea because AGE IS JUST AN ILLUSION!

You can be *Young* forever if you really want to. All you would have to do is use your IMAGINATION to feel young, and that will allow you to be young.

5) If you have not read Napoleon Hill's classic, *Think and Grow Rich*, then I highly endorse the book as a must-read for **Young Masterminds**. If you already have read the book, consider reading it again. Once is never enough for anything in life.

Chapter 5

Thinking to Grow Rich..?

"The world of things that come into being as a result of action, materializes through thinking"

-Ibn Khaldun

Do you think your thoughts can make your rich? I always wanted to grow rich, but I never knew I could think and grow rich. After extensively indulging in Bob Proctor's teachings, I realized that his normal life turned into a phenomenal life over the years due to the principles he had learned and applied from Napoleon Hill's book, *Think and Grow Rich*. The fascinating part is that Bob did not only read this book once; he read it every day for more than fifty-five years, and he still reads it till this very day. I **desired** to purchase this book but after taking a closer look at my mother's library, I realized that this book had been around me for years! My uncle in Canada, who is an entrepreneur, gifted the book to my dad and me several years earlier. Immediately my memory kicked in and I remembered reading the book on my way to school in the ninth grade. I couldn't even recall if I finished reading the entire book, but even if I did, I was a *Sleepwalker* who was unaware. This time I was keen to read this book with the *Conscious*

Awareness that I developed and then apply the principles of success in my life. The dots were slowly connecting, and my vision was getting clearer by the day. At that point in my life, I had fully acknowledged that my old ideas on how to grow rich were all negative false beliefs. If I wanted to be financially free the legal way, I had to learn how to *think* in a certain way. This may sound ridiculous, but the act of *thinking* is only done by a few people on this planet, and that is why genuinely successful people who live extraordinary lives are a minority in the human population only because they *think* in a certain way. George Bernard Shaw once said, *"Two percent of the people think; three percent of the people think they think, and ninety-five percent of the people would rather die than think."*

In Chapter 9, **Education as Entertainment**, I elaborate on this particular topic and explain how you can start thinking in a certain way.

Do you want to read a book that was read by more than 100 million human beings? I did, but I not only wanted to read *Think and Grow Rich*, I desired to read the exact same edition that Bob Proctor owns because I knew that it transformed his entire life and I believed that I would start *thinking* to grow rich if I read it as well. I researched online and realized that Napoleon Hill wrote the original book in 1937, but the one that I had at home was the 21st century updated edition. I also found out many other versions are missing some very important original content, so now I decided that I would not read it until I found the 1937 classic edition. On March 31st, 2016, I was at my best friend's house in Jeddah. We both were sitting on a comfortable leather couch watching a movie in his dad's luxurious living room, and out of nowhere I randomly started staring at the gigantic bookshelf behind me. I got distracted by the abundance of books and then I started scanning each shelf until I came across some interesting titles. I was an excited kid at a candy store who had a ***desire*** to learn the secrets to to success! I ended up borrowing three books to read over the spring break. These books were beneficial for my intellectual growth even though I was very new to the concept of personal development.

They included:

- *How Successful People Think* by John C. Maxwell

- *SUCCESS* - The Best of Napoleon Hill

- *The 10 Secrets of Entrepreneurs* by Keith C. Smith

Before I could get the opportunity to learn more from Bob Proctor and read *Think and Grow Rich*, I made up my mind to read these three books first. During my high school spring break, I started to wake up at 7 AM every morning and read on the roof of my house, while my family was asleep. I found peace and solitude up there because of the calming view of Arabian palm trees. I created a routine and started productively planning my day by the hour. After the three days of constant reading, I loved it, but I noticed that I wasn't able to remember every important idea from each chapter. Thanks to Abdul Lateef Jandali, also known as *Steve Jobs*, for using his imagination and creating the amazing iPhone, I came up with a creative solution to my dilemma. I started to use my iPhone 6 in a productive manner, by recording my myself reading important parts of select chapters. This method was a great way for backing up the knowledge to which I could later refer. When I came across long passages, I photographed the pages. These are the essential topics that left the most positive impact on my life.

How Successful People Think

- The right thought and the right people in the right environment at the right time for the right reason will yield the right result.

- Look for possibilities in every situation.

- Dream one size bigger.

- Set aside time for reflective thinking.

- Mediocre people follow the crowd and don't think for themselves.

Success: The Best of Napoleon Hill

- Education consists of doing not merely knowing.

- A definite chief aim in life consists of a purpose in life and a plan for attaining that purpose.

- Using your imagination is very important if you want to achieve anything in life.

- Mind your own business; it's your business to succeed in life.

- Over-deliver in the service you do, give more than you are paid for.

- Like people more than you like money.

- Failure is one of the most beneficial parts of a human being's experience.

The 10 Secrets of Entrepreneurs

- Successful entrepreneurs educate themselves more than they entertain themselves.

- Entrepreneurs are solution finders and employees are problem solvers.

- Successful entrepreneurs are willing to do what's hard now to make life easier later.

- Successful entrepreneurs hate complaining, employees love complaining.

- Successful entrepreneurs look in the future and employees look at the past.

- Successful entrepreneurs take risks because of faith, while employees play it safe because of the **F**alse **E**vidence **A**ppearing **R**eal. **(FEAR)**

After reading these three books, the book that left the most powerful impact on me was the *The 10 Secrets of Entrepreneurs* by Keith Cameron Smith. I resonated with this book quickly because ever since I was small, I have been an entrepreneur!

In middle school, I developed an interest in earning money, even though I received a monthly allowance from my parents. The friends I surrounded myself with, all had BlackBerry phones and eventually, I got influenced to *desire* my own phone. I wasn't working a job and I didn't want to just ask my parents to give me money so I started *thinking* in a certain way. I tapped into creative energy and it fuelled my desire to *think* of new ways where I could earn more money. Hence, my most vivid memory is of the fourth grade when I received a bundle of golden magnetic phonebook cards from a media sponsor at my mom's charity event for free. The quiet young entrepreneur in me decided to sell these cards to friends at school. I kept 100% of the profits since I had no overhead. Throughout middle school, my ideas expanded as I ventured further into the realm of business with the little knowledge I had. My products ranged from selling different candies at lunchtime and small trendy toys to headphones. For the latter, I found a wholesaler who had a retail shop and agreed to supply me with headphones at cost plus price, and I resold them to friends in school. The profit I made allowed me to reinvest in small business ideas or simply create savings.

The concepts of selling led me to self-awareness and forced me to enhance my communication and accounting skills. Dealing with potential customers improved my listening and persuasion capabilities dramatically, which in turn enhanced my performance at school. With a heightened sense of self-confidence, I took a challenge to create a neighborhood sale for kids. At first, I realized that there were many things in my house that were just taking up space and not being used so I thought of selling them like the way people do in Toronto. Since I didn't live in a typical Canadian neighborhood with garages, and I lived in a Saudi neighborhood without garages, I used my imagination to transform the idea of a classic garage sale into a "hallway sale". I sold this idea to kids in our condominium community by contacting a majority of the tenants to inquire if they would like me to sell any of their items on my table. The first venture was a success, and the sales were profitable for all parties. I hosted two more Hallway Sales in 2012 just for fun. Furthermore, I later tapped into the business segment of a leading trend, **Beats** headphones, which were very popular in those days. I took a leadership stance by training and assigning my friends to collect orders, perform door- to-door sales, and bring their orders with a detailed description to me by the end of the day. I would then go to 'my guy' that no one knew about and negotiate deals with the genuine intention to purchase headphones in bulk. This venture allowed me to generate massive profits for myself while being able to pay my friends that helped. At this point, I had more than enough money saved up to purchase a phone, but me always wanting to be unique and stand out from the crowd, I bought a touchscreen smartphone instead of a BlackBerry. Understand that I was able to attain my desire of owning a phone only because I took ACTION on my initial thought. I began *thinking* in a certain way, as this allowed me to accept the problem of not having my own phone and then *thinking* of the solution which was earning money. This thought turned into an idea because I really wanted a phone. If I didn't get obsessed with this desire, then I wouldn't have attracted the idea of earning money by selling. Although selling was not something I was used to, I got out of my comfort zone and took risks. The time, money and effort I invested in myself were completely worth the investment in the long run. If I didn't have the burning ***desire*** to purchase my own phone, then I wouldn't have been motivated to get up and take action every day!

Desire is the first lesson in *Think and Grow Rich* and it is the most important success principle for anyone who wants to live a happy, healthy and wealthy life. Understand that desire is the effort of the unexpressed possibility within your heart that is seeking to be expressed in your life by your actions. If you want the feeling of ***desire*** to always exist in you, then you must always have a continuous expectation for its fulfillment to take place regardless of any circumstances that seem negative and opposite of what you desire. Always remember that when you desire something to manifest, you should never expect in your heart for the opposite to happen because when you start expecting something you don't want, you end up attracting the undesirable into your life. On the other hand, if you want to attract your dreams into your reality then start expecting what you really want, and your ability to attract the desire becomes magnetic. Identify your ***desire*** and then expect it to come without needing to know exactly when, where, or how it will come into your life, all you have to do is be expectant with faith. The way will be shown. Just like all of the Universal Laws, the Law of Attraction is always in motion. You live in an ocean of motion and you are an emotional being. Energy plus motion equals e-motion. The Law of Attraction is an immutable natural law that responds to your emotions. You cannot choose to use this law one day and not use it the next day. This law is always working, and it's up to you to either work in harmony with the law or work against it. The choice is ultimately yours! All the successful people who experience a fulfilling life with an abundance of wealth, genuine happiness, lifelong health, true love, and serenity are only able to because they work in harmony with every Universal Law. There are 19 *Natural Laws of the Universe*, but below is a list of the most important laws.

1) Law of Perpetual Transmutation
2) Law of Relativity
3) Law of Vibration
4) Law of Polarity
5) Law of Rhythm
6) Law of Cause and Effect
7) Law of Gender

If you ***desire*** to learn how to master all these laws, then you are welcome to inquire about this upcoming certified program at the **Y**oung **M**asterminds **I**nstitute of **S**uccess.

One afternoon at a local bookstore, as I was skimming through the last aisle in the self-help section and right before I turned my head, shiny golden pages instantly caught my attention. I spotted with curiosity for a moment and gazed at the pages as if I just stopped hidden treasure. As I read the title on the black hardcover my pupils dilated with amazement and I couldn't believe that I actually found what I was seeking for all along!

THINK AND GROW RICH
THE COMPLETE CLASSIC TEXT

After consciously accepting the fact that I attracted what I desired into my life, I felt so happy and grateful. Then to express gratitude, I purchased another copy of this book for my best friend because giving a gift made me *feel* abundant at the moment.

"What you seek is seeking you."

- Rumi

Master Action Plan

1. Do you think it is possible to actually *'Think'* and **GROW** Rich?

If you believe you can, then why do you *desire* to grow rich? What do you really want to do with the riches?

2. What part of the population do you want to be a part of? Circle your answer

Remember that quote:

    a) 2% of the people think

    b) 3% of the people *think* they think

    c) 95% of the people would rather die than think

The Masterminding Experiment

Step 1:

Think of a friend you know who wants to be more positive and desires to live a successful life.

Step 2:

Once you have completely finished reading this book, you will naturally want to share it with others. So do that friend a favor and buy them a copy of this book, *'The Young Mastermind'*. If you want, you could tell them it's an early birthday gift.

Step 3:

After they finish reading this book, ask them what chapter shocked them the most. If their answer is **"Chapter 6"**, then that is the correct answer!

Step 4:

Observe their behavior and notice if your friend is trying to improve their life in any way possible…

Step 5: THIS PART IS FUN!

Follow up with your friend to see if they are planning to read *Think and Grow Rich*. If they eventually buy the book, that means your friend was serious about becoming very successful. On the other hand, if your friend finishes reading my book and they don't realize that they should read *Think and Grow Rich*, then that is a sign for you that maybe your friend is not seeking to be a part of the 2% of successful people who are able to actually THINK!

Chapter 6

Do What Successful People Do

"Where focus goes, energy flows"

-Tony Robbins

The formula for becoming successful is straightforward. If you do what successful people do, you can have what successful people have. At this point in my life, I fully realized that if I really wanted to become a successful person with a life full of abundance, then I would have to stop doing what the majority of people on this planet do. I would have to start doing what the minority of successful people do in order to live a happy, healthy, and wealthy life. Keith Cameron Smith said in his book,

"Successful entrepreneurs educate themselves more than they entertain themselves."

This statement was so accurate that it blew me away the moment I read it. I sat down alone in my room and started doing some deep thinking. I told myself that if I genuinely wanted to be rich in all areas of my life, then I would need to stop doing specific things. For example, I would have to stop watching stupid movies and negative news reports. I would have to stop listening to toxic music, wasting hours doing nothing in cafés, gossiping with friends, thinking and focusing on things that would never benefit me in the future, and associating with aimless people who lack a vision and a desire to be successful in all areas of life. Once I made the conscious decision to change my habitual activities, my whole life started to change! I then began to learn how to destroy negative habits with the guidance of my mentor, which in turn, allowed me to become aware of the fact that mainstream entertainment had been affecting my life in a harmful way as it was pulling me away from achieving my goals in life. Although I was raised in a positive environment, I was still exposed to forms of entertainment that painted the wrong picture of 'success'. Throughout my childhood, I was unconsciously programmed by movies, music, and video games. In fact, I now hold the firm belief that many of these forms of entertainment leave a negative influence on impressionable minds impacting their teenage years and adult lives. I used to be emotionally attached to three forms of entertainment: television, music, and video games.

The first form of entertainment were movies like *The Wolf of Wall Street, Jumper,* and *Scarface*, which presented a successful life with negative suggestions. I watched these movies time after time and enjoyed the storyline. The main characters of these movies influenced me in various ways. I desired the freedom that Jordan Belfort had to throw around cash at parties and blow money fast on useless stuff. I desired to be able to teleport like Jumper, live the "good life" and take shortcuts to success. I desired the lavish lifestyle like Tony Montana and reside in an opulent mansion with millions. The movie *Scarface* influenced me to such an extent that I learned how to imitate Tony Montana's Cuban accent and I memorized the exact lines of each character in the movie so I could act the famous scenes and have fun! These movies programmed my mind to believe in these false ideas; that in order to have a successful lifestyle with an abundance of time and money freedom, I would have to scam people by deceiving them on the idea that I would invest for them, but instead, I use their money to make money even more money for myself, become a Master Con-Artist to rob banks, and betray people for my own egotistical desires while dealing cocaine.

The second form of entertainment that influenced me in a negative way was music. I used to enjoy watching music videos that showed fancy cars, luxurious houses, cash, and women. This form of entertainment suggested to my mind that in order to achieve this lifestyle I needed weapons, be in constant conflict with police, dress in a certain way, be a womanizer, consume drugs and alcohol to feel happy.

The third form of entertainment I was addicted to was video games. I loved playing *Grand Theft Auto*. All the kids my age and older were playing it, which made it easy for me to manoeuver my way into playing it and eventually owning my secret copy of the game. Since the third grade, I was attracted to this game due to the illusion of freedom it gave me. In this game, players get the opportunity to experience the 'successful life' with all the luxuries, but in order to own any type of supercar, live in massive estates, fly a private jet, purchase exorbitant clothing or do ANYTHING the player desires, they must earn money. To earn money, players need to do specific missions that they are instructed to do by mafia bosses and gangsters. The game literally programs a player's mind to accept and believe that hijacking planes, robbing jewelry stores, killing fellow and rival gang members, stealing cars, blowing up police stations, and burning homes are things one must do in order to get rich and live the fictional 'successful life'. This may sound ridiculous to you, but once the gamer, movie watcher, or song lover gets emotionally attached to either form of entertainment, they start becoming programmed to think and accept these false ideas without even realizing it due to repetitive exposure. By Googling *"News reports of Grand Theft Auto in real life,"* you will come across hundreds of official stories that mention people of all ages who get arrested for committing crimes that resemble the behavior of missions in the video game. According to social scientists, video games influence crime in general. Some of the individuals who got arrested for doing dangerous, destructive things have been subconsciously programmed to move into action and do similar activities due to negative environmental programming. According to the American Psychological Association, *"...research demonstrates a consistent relation between violent video games and aggressive effect, and decreases in prosocial behavior."* Hence, any suggestions that violent videos games put out, which are unconsciously accepted into a player's mind over a period of time of constant playing, can potentially result in real life crimes. Many people play violent video games and do not commit crimes, and that is because they consciously reject the negative suggestions in the game from programming their subconscious mind. The important lesson here is to avoid accepting what is portrayed in violent video games and replace negative forms of entertainment with positive forms of entertainment.

Do you understand exactly how these forms of entertainment program a person's mind in a subliminal way that negatively impacts a person's success in life? I assume you've heard of this common expression at some point in your life, *"a baby's mind is like a tape recording machine."* Understand that anything a child experiences with their five senses automatically gets programmed into the child's subconscious mind. From birth until the age of seven, the subconscious is entirely open to ANY suggestions. Everything parents, family, or teachers believe and teach to a child is programmed into the child's subconscious mind. Any idea a child is exposed to through their five senses gets directly planted into the subconscious. For example, hate for onions or broccoli, speaking in a particular way, use of the right hand to eat instead of the left are things a person does because their parents did and still may do, but that person is usually doing things habitually without even acknowledging it. According to Bob Proctor, this is called **environmental programming**. This type of programming is inevitable, but a person's environment may not always be positive and success orientated. In addition to environmental programming, people are also genetically programmed. This is why you may look similar to other members of your family: you share genes. For most people, the age of seven is when things start to change in the brain. At the age of five, six, or seven, a child develops the ability to think because the conscious mind has evolved to that point. The conscious mind is the intellectual part of the human personality, it has a reasoning faculty, which is why children go through a phase of asking their parents interesting questions that begin with **"Why."** From the age of seven onward, the conscious mind has the power and ability to either *accept* or *reject* any idea. This is why the older a child gets, the harder it is for the parent(s) to convince the child to believe in stories like the tooth fairy, Santa Claus or the big monster under the bed. The reasoning faculty allows your mind to *think* for yourself and not depend on other people's thoughts to affect you.

Did you ever wonder how thoughts form in your mind or how you are even able to THINK a *thought?* It's very simple...

ARE YOU READY TO GET MINDBLOWN?

I assume you are a human. That means you are the Creator's highest form of creation. Why? Because you along with billions of other human beings are the only creature on planet earth, who has the power and ability to *think* in a certain way. So back to my question. Did you ever wonder how thoughts form in your mind?

*Take a moment to THINK right now by
breathing in and out deeply...*

YOU are conditioned to THINK with your five senses. Thoughts usually come from something perceived by the senses, that is, seen, smelled, tasted, touched, or heard. When someone says anything to you, you start to question whether it is correct or incorrect using the reasoning faculty of your conscious mind. So your conscious mind has the freedom to either accept or reject a thought. If the conscious mind accepts a thought, you naturally start to believe it. When the thought has been accepted by your conscious mind, it is passed down to your subconscious mind. The subconscious is the emotional part of the human personality and has NO ability to reject any thought. It accepts whatever thought is impressed upon it. The interesting part is that your subconscious cannot tell the difference between reality and imagination. On the other hand, when a thought is presented to your mind, and you choose not to believe in it, your conscious mind immediately rejects that thought, and nothing happens because your subconscious mind doesn't get affected in any way.

Did you know that once upon a time, Muhammad Ali **thought** he could actually become the most successful boxer ever? He converted this thought into an idea because his conscious mind accepted this thought. Ali started to tell himself, "I AM THE GREATEST!" He had a burning *desire* to become the greatest boxer of all time, so naturally, he started to believe in this idea so much that his conscious mind accepted this thought and naturally passed it down to his subconscious mind. His subconscious immediately accepted the idea, as it had no ability to reject the idea. Whenever Ali imagined that he was already the greatest boxer of all time, his subconscious thought that what he's imagining is an actual hard fact in his own perceived 'reality'. Ali got obsessed with living his dream life that he repeated this phrase so many times throughout his career, especially before his boxing matches, that it eventually became his physical reality. Muhammad Ali manifested his dream by becoming the

'GREATEST BOXER OF ALL TIME'.
This chapter is the climax of this book, and if you pay very close attention to the rest of this section, you will learn how to literally attract ANYTHING you REALLY want to accomplish in your life with the power of your MIND! Now I will explain in further detail how the *Master Power of Spoken Word* allowed Muhammad Ali to manifest his life's desire.

The human body from neck to toe is just an instrument of the mind as it obeys the subconscious. The subconscious mind attentively listens to any suggestions that are made. Muhammad Ali originated the idea: "I AM THE GREATEST" and dreamed of converting the idea of becoming the greatest boxer of all time into a hard fact. He then got emotionally involved with this worthy ideal through repetition as he started believing that what he wanted was already his. This manifestation process impressed his burning ***desire*** upon his subconscious mind. The subconscious then commanded his body to move into action, which caused a reaction, that led to an attraction of transforming him into the greatest boxer of all time. He used to be an average boxer, but he transformed into the greatest because he chose to believe in the idea of becoming **'THE GREATEST'**. Ali wouldn't have become the greatest if he didn't THINK that thought. That thought only became a reality because he got obsessed with his dream. This is how Muhammad Ali's subconscious mind automatically commanded his body to do the necessary actions that would get him to his goal.

One of the Natural Laws of the Universe is the Law of ***Cause*** and *Effect*. This law states that whatever you send out into the universe must come back to you. Action and Re-action are equal and opposite. So if you think, feel, or do something, it will automatically come back to you, regardless if it is positive or negative. So Muhammad Ali held on to his dream on the screen of his mind with faith and certainty, and that was the *Cause*. Since his subconscious mind commanded his body to move into **ACTION**, his body was motivated to work hard every day and master the required skills through extensive training. The desired result he attracted into his life was being recognized all over the world as the 'GREATEST BOXER OF ALL TIME', and this was the *Effect*. If you already registered for the *Master Power of Spoken Program*, then you are aware of how he installed this affirmation into his mind with the unique Kinesiology method. When people asked about how Muhammad Ali became the 'GREATEST' he replied honestly by saying, *"It's the repetition of affirmations that leads to belief. And once that belief becomes a deep conviction, things begin to happen."*

Please put your focused attention towards understanding the following paragraphs even though it may sound easy because the information that you are going to learn is extremely powerful and immensely valuable for you to become the Master of Your Own Mind.

I want YOU to ask yourself this question:
How does a baby seed transform into a plant?

If you weren't skipping class in the first grade, then you would be aware of this process. To successfully plant a seed in a garden, sunlight and water are required in order for that baby seed to grow into a beautiful plant. I am now going to illustrate how you can create your desired dream life just by planting seeds in your mind. As you read on, let your imagination run wild!

Consider a seed to be any positive idea/goal/desire or a dream that you really WANT to accomplish in your life. First, you must **BELIEVE** that you can achieve it no matter how *'impossible'* it may seem to attain. Now to plant this seed you need soil, so consider the soil/ garden to be your subconscious mind. Next, you need sunlight for the seed to grow, so consider the Sun's rays to be your positive emotions of just feeling better than ever! Lastly, to make sure this seed grows into a plant, you need water. Consider droplets of water to be the act of repetition. Remember this: Any seed in the garden can grow only **IF** you provide enough sunlight and water.

Master Ingredients For Success

Soil = your subconscious mind (garden)

Seed = desire (idea)

Sunlight = feeling really good! (positive emotions)

Water = the act of repetition (over and over)

If you want to manifest any desire or you want to convert your dream into a reality, or you want to accomplish a particular goal, then below is the step by step process on exactly how you can make things happen with the power of your mind. There is only one way, and now you have access to this golden way!

WARNING: DON'T FOLLOW THE INSTRUCTIONS IF YOU AREN'T SERIOUS ABOUT SUCCESS. IF YOU ARE SERIOUS, THEN DON'T JUST READ, ACTUALLY DO THEM.

The Master Manifestation Method

SOIL

Understand that your subconscious mind is the garden of your mind. YOU have an abundance of soil in this part of your mind and you have the freedom to plant ANYTHING you desire.

SEED

Step 1: THINK of something you *really really* WANT to attract into your life.

Step 2: Write out exactly what you desire to have on a piece of paper in detail. Do NOT write it on your phone, laptop, iPad or any device.

SUNLIGHT

Step 3: Ask yourself if you genuinely *believe* that YOU can actually have what you desire?

Step 4: If you want to attract your desire you <u>MUST</u> *Believe* that it is <u>POSSIBLE</u>, otherwise this will **NOT** work. If it is hard to believe at first, play a game with our mind and *act* like you DO believe in something…

Step 5: Now that you *Believe* in yourself, and feel like you can actually have what you WANT, close your eyes.

Step 6: See yourself on the screen of your mind already in possession of your desire. You can do this also by imagining yourself sitting in a movie theatre and watching your dream life on the big screen.

Step 7: VISUALIZE and **FEEL** like the thing(s) you DESIRE to have is already yours. Picture yourself living the life you really want to live, doing the things you really want to do, experiencing life the way really you wish to, owning what you really want to have. Use your five senses to actually feel as if what you are imagining is your physical reality right NOW.

Let your IMAGINATION run wild so your subconscious mind can think that what you are seeing in your mind is actually true and your life is this way at this very moment.

Step 8: It may be difficult to convince yourself that what you are seeing is REAL, but you must tell yourself that YOU are an actor or an actress that is getting paid to ACT in a film and you have no choice but to *act* that what you are seeing in your imagination is REAL. Use this analogy to convince yourself to believe as if what you are seeing is your actual *'reality'*. If you do this specific activity often, your big dream will eventually become your actual reality!

Steps 3-8 - are the roles of Sunlight in this process. Remember *feeling* the positive emotions is the most important part of the **Master Manifestation Method**.

WATER

Step 9: If you have access to a mirror, that is great! If not, then you can use a front-facing camera. If you aren't able to see your own reflection then you can still do this activity, but this process will work even more powerfully when you can see yourself.

Step 10: Create a **M**aster **A**ffirmation

This is an example of a Master Affirmation: *I'm so happy and grateful now that...I am a happy, healthy and wealthy person.*

You can begin writing your affirmation like this:

I'm so happy and grateful now that...

_____

_____

_____

Write down anything you dream of having on a piece of paper. Write this in the present tense as if you already have what you **desire**.

Step 11: Repetition is extremely important. Once you have written down your own **M**aster **A**ffirmation, then you must start repeating this affirmation over and over every single day. You have to say it to yourself at least once a day. If you can see the reflection of your face, then look at yourself and repeat the statement as much as you can until it becomes an automatic habit for you.

Step 12: Every time you say this affirmation to yourself or while you look at yourself in the mirror, you must genuinely BELIEVE what you are saying. You have to feel like what you are saying is an actual FACT. If you just say it without feeling the *'reality'* of it, then it will **NOT** manifest and you won't be able to attract what you desire into your life.

In a matter of time, your dream, goal or idea will start to move into physical form and transform from an idea into an actual reality. Once your desire manifests in your life, that means the baby seed has successfully grown into a beautiful plant.

Understand that if you can see what you want in your mind's eye, then you can see it with your actual eyes! Your body is simply an instrument of your mind. Whatever your mind says, your body listens to carefully and performs it in a corresponding behavior. Your body responds with an action that causes a re-action in the universe, and that automatically sets up a force of attraction which then manifests your desired result. This is also known as the Law of Attraction. If you watched *The Secret* movie, you would recall these steps: Ask, Believe and Recieve. The problem is that if you really want this process to work for you then you cannot skip the most important step: **The Master Attitude of Gratitude.**

Giving thanks is the real secret that most people forget about. The common person experiences 'life' without expressing enough gratitude. Understand that no matter how much thanks you give, there are trillions of things in your whole life to be grateful for and even if you try to count how many things you should feel grateful for, you will never end up finishing, because whether you are aware of all the blessing or not, there are an eternal amount of blessings in your life since you were born with *Infinite Potential*. YOU are always manifesting things in your life, eihter consciously or unconsciously. Every day you may have positive experiences or negative experiences, but the fact of the matter is, you are 100% responsible for every single thing that happens in your life because it all comes back to your state of thinking. Did you know *sound* directly affects your life? Whatever you think, feel to be true and say, whether positive or negative, you end up attracting into your life. This is an immutable natural law of the universe. Just keep in mind, thoughts are things!

To return to the third form of entertainment, I mentioned at the beginning of this chapter by which I was influenced: music.

I developed an in-depth understanding of the subconscious and became more aware of its infinite potential after reading *The Power of Your Subconscious Mind* by Dr. Joseph Murphy. At the end of my last year in high school, I started paying attention to the sounds I allowed my mind to be exposed to every day. This interest led to the point where I discovered how music had been affecting my life for years. I used to listen to music many times throughout my day, including in the early morning and the evening before I went to sleep. It is scientifically proven the subconscious is extremely receptive to any suggestions 15 minutes after waking up and before falling asleep. This is when the mind is in a drowsy state and not completely alert. The correct terminology for this state is the Alpha level of mind. Unfortunately, I was programming my own mind and then attracting undesirable results in my life due to repetitive exposure from harmful lyrics. Since I was a *Sleepwalker*, I was unaware of this truth, even though my parents used to tell me, *"the music you listen to is not really healthy for your brain.."* Once my mind reached a higher level of *Conscious Awareness*, I realized that my parents were right all along. I began paying more attention to the lyrics of certain songs on the radio and noticed that a lot of songs were full of screaming, swearing, abusing, cheating, arguing, manipulating etc. I then realized that these songs were not designed to bring out the best version of myself or promote growth.

My best friend and I used to love listening to Rap, Hip-Hop, R&B and enjoyed Rock, House, Trap, Heavy Metal, and Reggae. The lyrics in songs made us feel good because we could connect on an emotional level, but we paid more attention to what resonated with us the most: the driving force behind the lyrics. We realized that after listening to many songs over and over again, we stopped paying attention to the real meaning behind each lyric because our minds' were focused on waiting for the beat to drop in a song. Most people get excited about the beat drop in a song because the moment the beat drops the human brain gets stimulated, and happy hormones are released. We then noticed that once the rhythm in a song reached its peak, the lyrics began to fade away from our conscious attention. This created a trance-like state where the lyrics and the rhythm of a song blended as one. We then became aware of the fact that we were planting many negative ideas (seeds) in the garden of our minds (subconscious) every time we listened to a particular song more than once. We then figured out how a majority of mainstream songs have at least one lyric that contains a negative suggestion in any context. The sad truth is that these negative ideas/ suggestions are embedded within the lyrics, and it's hard to recognize them the first time a song is played. At this point in our lives, we both had been exposed to hundreds of negative ideas because for many years we listened to songs with harmful lyrics more than once and got emotionally involved with the songs. After we listened to particular songs for a long period of time, our minds' naturally started to believe in the ideas that were suggested throughout the lyrics. Any form of repetition that is done on the conscious level eventually reaches the subconscious level, and if there is emotion in the repetition of ideas, the subconscious mind immediately gets programmed and then commands the body to act upon the suggested ideas. Since we allowed our minds' to hear these harmful lyrics more than once, our subconscious had been negatively programmed.

This programming controlled our thoughts, feelings, and actions which caused us to **desire** a life that represented the negative ideas in the lyrics of songs. The effect of listening to harmful lyrics was a drastic change in our behavior. The music videos influenced us to such an extent that we started to walk, dress, and speak like the artists' who we looked up to. The end result was that we attracted negative outcomes in our lives because our moods were impacted by these sounds. The root cause of destructive behavior was our minds' being exposed to low vibration music.

Did you know the beat, rhythm, chorus or hook of a song creates an impact on your emotional state which in turn affects your mood? As you know, everything is *energy*, and the new 'cool way' people refer to energy is a *vibe*. The word emotion is a combination of two words Energy + Motion = E-Motion. The state of energy your body is in at any moment is called a *vibration*. So when an artist creates a song, the artist's emotional state is transmitted into the recording. This directly influences and effects the vibration of a song. When you press the play button, the energy in any song directly affects your mood, because your mind is exposed to the same exact vibration. One of the Natural Laws of the Universe is the Law of Vibration. This law states that every single thing in this universe *vibrates*, nothing is sitting still in its place. Being consciously aware of a vibration is called *feeling*. Music is so powerful that it can either make you *feel* positive or *feel* negative because any song has the ability to change your *feelings* due to its trance effect on the mind.

IMAGINE you are listening to a new song that your friend told you about. In the beginning, you don't resonate with the song too much but after listening to more than once you start enjoying it. Remember how I explained that your subconscious is the emotional part of your personality, so naturally, your mind is inclined to love the sound of a song. Now while the song is playing, each lyric is either suggesting a positive or negative idea and since you are being entertained by the sound, your conscious mind (the door to your subconscious) is left wide open to **ANY** suggested idea. This is why it accepts the positive or negative ideas contained within the lyrics and then all ideas get passed down to your subconscious mind. When you continue to listen to any song more than once, you are exposed to the same vibration, and that has a significant effect on your subconscious. When YOU are <u>unaware</u> of a vibration, your mind is greatly impacted far more than normal because it is vulnerable to outside vibrations.

Repetitive exposure to the sounds and lyrics of songs will eventually ***attract*** whatever is suggested in the song into your life! This inevitably happens due to the fact that your subconscious mind is not able to reject ideas because it only accepts ideas, images or sounds that are impressed upon it. So regardless whether the ideas in lyrics are positive or negative, they are bound to impact the quality of your life since they naturally get planted into the garden of your mind. This garden is your subconscious mind, and it commands your body to move into *action*, which then causes a *reaction,* and this starts to create the *attraction*. Before I go any further, I must elaborate on the power of sound and its influence on your life.

Can you estimate how much water your human body contains? According to a study performed by H.H. Mitchell, published in the Journal of Biological Chemistry, the amount of water in the skin is 64%, lungs are 83%, muscles and kidneys are 79%, bones are 31%, heart and brain is 73%. This demonstrates that every single cell in your body has a high consistency of water. Scientifically, when sound waves reach a liquid surface, they transform the water molecules into either a structured geometrical pattern or a distorted form. The transformation varies depending on the sound's vibrational frequency.

Dr. Masaru Emoto, a leading Japanese researcher, studied the effects of human consciousness on water. The study provides visual proof of how human thoughts, ideas, words, and sounds impact water consciousness. His fascinating research demonstrated that water's physical appearance is not the only visible change; rather the actual molecular structure of water entirely changes!

Furthermore, a renowned French doctor, Alfred Tomatis, spent many years researching sacred sounds from around the world. His research includes particularly sacred chanting from Tibetan, Gregorian, Islamic, and Jewish traditions. Tomatis found that many of the sacred sounds on the planet are rich in high frequency called harmonics and believes that these sounds like a battery, charge the cortex of the brain and stimulate health and wellness for an overall harmonious state of being. Similarly, the sounds emitted through chants from sacred text recitals like a recitation of verses from the Holy Quran, impact the molecular structure of water creating beautiful geometrical shaped crystals. Likewise, this effect is produced through classical music in contrast to heavy metal where crystals appear shapeless, rather deformed. This proves that *sound* itself is the most potent form of energy you can receive or send out at any time.

This proves that when you are exposed to high pitch intense sounds, such as loud noise, screaming, machinery, rock, heavy metal music, and negative words or ideas, the crystal formations of water in your body become shapeless and distorted. On the other hand, when you are exposed to positive calming sounds, ideas, or words, the crystal formations of water in your body become beautiful like snowflakes. Now imagine how impactful thoughts, ideas, words, and sounds have on YOU because your body is predominantly water! This shows why you **MUST** make a conscious effort on being aware of the ideas you choose to accept, the thoughts you choose to think, the words you choose to say, and the sounds you choose to listen to since they inevitably shape your life!

As a result of this awareness, I was curious to know how many negative suggestions each song had and I wanted to consciously hear the lyrics that had been entering my mind every day. I convinced my best friend to sit down with me in his car to conduct an experiment by scanning the lyrics of our favorite songs. Like scientists, we played each song aloud and dissected the lyrics word by word. As soon as we heard a negative idea in a lyric, we noticed a pattern of suggestions. The most common ideas we found were: being broke for life, using women as objects and harassing them, being addicted to drugs is cool, the benefit of crime, cheating on a partner for lust, staying depressed for no real reason, murdering family members over jealousy, the unnecessary use of weapons, living in jail, drug dealing to make a fortune, burning money to show off, stealing jewelry, and other harmful ideas in the lyrics of millions of famous songs. Our discovery shocked us and brought us to the realization that we along with billions of humans all over the world were being negatively programmed for years! Taking immediate action, we then deleted the majority of songs from our playlists. Deep down we both knew for a fact that some songs were counterproductive to our success, but we had let our moral guard down and considered such songs to be *'harmless'*.

In contrast, there are several artists throughout the music industry who choose to create songs with a meaningful message. These artist's intentions' are to benefit the listener by adding positive suggested ideas in their lyrics rather than negative ideas. After deleting the majority of my songs, I still left a few that I was very attached to. As I continued to improve my life by learning new things, my level of *Conscious Awareness* increased and whenever I played my favorite songs, I would somehow spot at least more than one lyric in the song that contained a negative idea. Although I didn't have the courage to remove that song from my playlist I knew my mind was getting programmed to accept and believe in the suggestions because of repetitive listening. It got to the point where I would be able to realize how I attracted something positive or negative in my day and then I could trace the attraction back to where the first thought was created. Now I still desired to listen to mainstream music because the *sound* in the songs made me feel really good as it stimulated my brain, but I realized that sounds in songs create strong feelings of attachment that no matter how many negative ideas or self-destructive messages are in the lyrics, I still wanted to listen because I slightly felt addicted to the *sound*.

Furthermore, I found a solution to this problem. I began listening to instrumental versions of all my favorite songs as there were no lyrics, my mind couldn't get programmed in a negative way. One day my older cousin, Yusuf told me about this entrepreneurship channel on youtube by the name of *Evan Carmichael*. I found a playlist that was titled,"Productive Music" and each month a new playlist is uploaded with different content. As I listened to the hour-long audio, I started to feel the same feelings that stimulated my brain. Evan removes all the lyrics and keeps the beat with all sounds of each song. The cool thing is that he does this for famous and classic songs that everyone loves in all genres. I am forever grateful to Evan for creating phenomenal content because thanks to him my problem is solved. I no longer wanted to listen to harmful lyrics that programmed my mind in a negative way, because I got the same feeling just by listening to the *sound* of songs! I dare you to try this and see how you feel. I'd be happy if it helps you!

My old friends that I no longer surrounded myself with would dedicate an entire day to listen to a brand new album, while I would dedicate my day to reading books and listening to audio recordings on success. I knew people who used to spend thousands of dollars to go to a famous concert with backstage passes. I put myself in their shoes, and after coming into higher a state of *Conscious Awareness*, I simply couldn't imagine myself working around the clock, then using the money I earned to purchase concert tickets to enter a low vibrational environment. Then be negatively programmed for hours while meeting the artist responsible for this self-destructive behavior and beg them for a selfie! Rather, what I would do with that money, is enter a high vibrational environment like a personal development seminar to learn from the most successful humans on earth! At a seminar, I would receive invaluable knowledge, and gain insight on how to improve my life intellectually, spiritually, physically, emotionally, financially and socially from a mentor(s).

Understand that your mind is like a garden and you can plant negative or positive seeds in your mind. Remember seeds are ideas (thoughts). The garden of your mind doesn't care what you plant, it makes sure all seeds grow into plants. In other words, your subconscious mind manifests any thought or idea into physical reality whether you are aware of it happening or not. This is how the creative process works for humans, and it is always working by universal law. If you feel good while listening to a song, that means you are in tune with the lyrics on an emotional level and at least one negative idea from the song can get directly planted into your subconscious mind. This is how you can end up attracting any negative result into your life just by using your ears.

My *desire* for riches was still alive but my mind was programmed by all these forms of entertainment to believe 'success' is a life full of materialistic luxuries, exotic drugs, and violence and in order to obtain such a lifestyle I would have to commit some sort of crime. These forms of entertainment painted the exact opposite picture of genuine success.

I, Muhammad Ali, still enjoy listening to music and I always will as life without sound is dull. I choose to only listen to sounds that make me feel good without depending on lyrics as I'm **NOT** interested in negatively programming my mind because it is the most valuable asset I have as a human. However, I choose to listen to many forms of music in different genres that have lyrics which contain positive suggestions instead of negative.

At the end of the day, I am so happy and grateful now that famous music artists, movie producers, and video game programmers are improving their content with the genuine intention to spread positivity through these forms of entertainment. Thank you for allowing yourself to reach this point of the book. I assume you might be shocked, excited, or even confused, don't worry because you are on the right path. Please remember that on the ***'Acknowledgments'*** page, you will be provided with the details on how to access your FREE *Master Manifestation Method* Video Program. There is a direct link to this course on the last page of this book.

Now that you are aware of *Do What Successful People Do*, there is one more thing you need to do before you can learn how to create your mirror to success.

Finish the **Master Action Plan** for this chapter!

Master Action Plan

1. Think of all the forms of entertainment that you have been exposed to from the time you were a kid to where you are now. Make a list of each and every form of negative entertainment that you believe programmed your mind in a destructive way.

2. If you truly want to become a successful person who lives a happy, healthy and wealthy life, then are you WILLING to educate yourself more than entertain yourself? Make a DECISION right now that you are "willing to educate yourself more than entertain youself."

3. Are you going to take out time to scan the lyrics of the songs you listen to, so you can become aware of the suggestions within the lyrics?

Try this experiment of scanning all the song's lyrics in your playlists. Imagine you are listening to each song for the first time and all you are going to do is be judgemental. Then just ignore the sound and try your best to focus on understanding the meaning behind each lyric. As soon as you recognize a negative suggestion, press pause and ask yourself if you want to attract what the lyric is suggesting into your own life. At first, you may say to yourself, *"ohh its just one negative lyric, it won't affect me, I'll ignore it."*, continue to play the song and you will soon notice that most songs have at least more than one negative suggestion in any context. It all depends on how much focused attention you direct towards understanding the real meaning behind each and every single lyric.

Write down your name and choose what day you are going to do this productive activity.

I do _____ will dedicate my time to this Master Activity on _____

4. After reading all the detailed information about your own mind in this long chapter, explain in your own words exactly what you understood about the infinite potential power in your mind.

5. Do you understand the concept of how your mind is like a garden and how you have the power to create ANYTHING you want in life just by planting seeds in your subconscious mind?

If you don't completely understand this truth to life, thats normal because when I first learned about the unique power of my conscious and subconscious mind, I was grateful but I did not fully understand it, so I studied even more and I always will.

I highly suggest that YOU read **this chapter** as many times as you need until you are able to explain the real power of the mind to someone else.

Chapter 7

The Mirror to Success

"Your most important sale in life is to sell yourself to yourself."

-Maxwell Maltz

Did you know all human beings on the face of this eath carry an image of themselves in their marvelous minds? This image is called the *Self-Image*.

For eighteen years, I was walking around with an image of myself, in my subconscious mind, and I didn't even realize it. I used to be an introverted person until the age of fifteen because I unconsciously held an image of myself in my mind as *'shy'*. Remember the popular kid at school who was good with teachers and had many friends? That person was not only confident on the outside but the inside as well. All extroverted people have an image in their mind of confidence, and they firmly believe they are confident, regardless if they are aware of their image or not. The common term for this is selfesteem. My self-image began to change as I got out of my comfort zone and talked more in public. Over the years I transformed that *'shy'* image into a *'dominant'* image which was full of confidence. Now I have the ability to speak in front of large audiences all around the world without experiencing any shyness because I no longer hold that same image of myself in my mind. Let me share an interesting funny story with you first before I show you how to create your mirror to success!

Throughout my childhood, I was a sneaky kid who used to get away with mischief, but over the years I got better at doing things behind my parents' back. The act of deceiving my parents became easier because I conditioned myself by watching movies and TV shows where young actors were talented at getting away with doing bad things by deceiving others. At the time I wasn't aware how these forms of entertainment were changing my self-image in my subconscious mind. The first time I watched the movie, *Agent Cody Banks*, I carefully observed his actions because I wanted to become like him. I desired to be hired by an intelligence organization and go on missions as a young spy like Agent Cody so I could feel 'successful'. I must've watched the movie *Home Alone* hundreds of times throughout the years. Due to repetitive watching, my subconscious mind got programmed, and I desired to set up unique traps and be extremely street smart like Kevin McCallister. After watching Disney's TV series, *The Suite Life of Zack & Cody*, I desired to do crazy things with my best friend and get away with trouble just like the hotel twins did. The video game *Hitman* was one of my favorite video games to play in my teenage years. I loved the feeling of almost getting caught by authority but escaping at the last second and hiding in closets. The whole concept of taking risks is what stimulated my mind. I got emotionally attached to these fictional characters, their unique abilities, and their 'successful' lifestyles. This resulted in me unconsciously creating an image of myself being able to do and accomplish what these characters did. I ended up attracting similar situations in my life that led me to develop those habits, skills, and characteristics.

In contrast, there were forms of entertainment that programmed my subconscious mind in a positive way. Throughout my childhood, I loved watching animated tv series like the *Magic School Bus*, *Arthur*, and *George Shrinks*. I was recently curious to understand what my mind had been exposed to at the very early stages of my life. As I rewatched a few episodes from these three shows, I recognized positive messages in the theme song of *Arthur* such as: "..its a wonderful day today..., listen to heart..listen to the beat, ...believe in yourself and that's the way to start!". Due to listening to these lyrics hundreds of times, all the suggestions got planted into the garden on my mind and formed a positive Self-Image. The famous cartoon, *Magic School Bus* made me feel that school can be fun if I use my imagination to make it fun. I expand more on this in the upcoming chapter. If you ever watched the unique cartoon *George Shrinks*, you would be more creative than you already are because the overall storyline sparks creativity! In Disney's *Wizards of Waverly Place*, there are multiple positive and negative subliminal messages that influence the viewer's mind. Go listen to Selena Gomez sing the show's theme song and try to see if your mind can pick up all the positive lyrics that have a deeper meaning to them. I genuinely believe these shows and cartoons programmed my subconscious which impacted my life in many positive ways and I'm grateful to the human beings who thought of creating impactful content.

To effectively explain the mirror to success, I must share what I learned from Bob Proctor's lecture titled, "Self-Image in 5 minutes". If you have a negative image of yourself, then that is because you have accepted false information about yourself as true. Around 1960, Dr. Maxwell Maltz wrote the book *Psycho-Cybernetics*. Cybernetics is the science of control and communication in animals and machines. It measures deviation from a goal, sends information to a coordinating mechanism that corrects the output, and keeps whatever it is moving toward the set goal. Now, IMAGINE that YOU are on an airplane that is taking you from New York to Dubai. The pilot starts feeling tired and chooses to turn on the *auto-pilot* mode. Understand this mode is a cybernetic instrument. This *auto-pilot* mode now follows the route to Dubai which is programmed into the plane's computer operating system. Then, IMAGINE out of nowhere the plane starts to shake, and immediately you hear the flight attendant's voice. She announces that there is turbulence due to the heavy weather conditions, and the plane goes off the programmed route for some time. This causes the cybernetic instrument in the plane's *auto-pilot* mode to quickly detect the plane is gone off its programmed route. It then measures the deviation from the set goal of arriving in Dubai and communicates to the wings of the plane to move in a particular direction. The plane automatically starts moving back to the programmed route and the flight pattern is then corrected. Now the plane you were sitting on in your imagination will successfully arrive in Dubai as intended thanks to the cybernetic instrument.

Did you know that your subconscious mind has a cybernetic instrument just like the *auto-pilot* mode of a plane? The cybernetic instrument in your mind is called the *Self-Image*. The self-image controls your entire life because you become what you think about and you are- what you do. Habitual behavior perpetuates itself. If you don't like the results you are currently getting in your life, then you should take a look at your habits. If you want to become excellent at everything in life, then your habits must be excellent.

> *"We are what we repeatedly do. Excellence, then, is not an act, but a habit."*
>
> -Aristotle

Why do you brush your teeth every morning after waking up? If you are one of the people on the planet who brush their teeth, it is because the idea of brushing your teeth was planted in your subconscious at a very young age, and once you accepted it, you started doing it without giving it any conscious thought. After brushing your teeth for a couple of months, the act of brushing became a natural habit. Most likely, you don't even really *think* about brushing your teeth now; you just do it. Your body performs this automatic behavior because the act of brushing is ingrained in your mind. Likewise, your self-image is also located in your subconscious mind. Remember the subconscious is the emotional part of the mind that controls your behavior which leads to every result you attract into your life. If your self-image is programmed in a certain way, then you are always going to be going in that particular direction out of habit. Your body is programmed to do a habitual action automatically because it has been doing the same action for years. At the end of the day, habits are incredibly powerful. You have the choice to either be an extraordinary person who has Mastermind habits or an ordinary person who has Mediocre habits. The choice is ultimately yours! If you would like the official step by step guide on how to master your habitual behavior and break negative patterns, then you can download the FREE report here: www.TheYoungMastermind.com/Habits

> *"Successful people are simply those with successful habits."*
>
> - Brian Tracy

Were you ever curious to know why only a few students always got good grades in school and why the rest didn't? Throughout my years of traditional education, a terror barrier was holding me back. This barrier didn't allow me to excel in my grades. The first time I was able to comprehend that my science grade was a *'C,'* was the same time my Self-Image for a school grade was created. The letter *'C'* has no meaning to me now, but it once meant that I was NOT smart. My teachers never suggested that I wasn't smart, but the letter itself suggested to my mind that I didn't have something that another student who received an *'A'* in science had. Deep down I enjoyed the subject of science, and at times I did put in the genuine effort, but my science grades were always in the *'C'* category. The *Conscious Awareness* that I developed has allowed me to understand why I always received a *'C'* grade in a subject that I enjoyed. The first time I acknowledged that my final grade in science was a *'C,'* an image immediately popped up in my mind of me not being a smart kid. I accepted this image because the report card was not a prank from my school, it was my final grade, so I had no choice but to believe that this grade represented me. The years went by, and I kept on getting below average grades. However, I vividly recall the end of seventh grade, because my final grade in physics turned out to be an *'A.'*

I will always be grateful to my dad for tutoring me since the first grade because he taught me everything there was to know on the subject of physics and that allowed me to have the confidence to ace the exam which resulted in me receiving 97% as my final grade. I was astonished when I heard my teacher congratulate me in front of the whole class, but I was confused at the same time. The following year my grade in physics was back to a *'C'* grade. I experienced this downfall mainly because from a very early age I had unknowingly accepted an image of myself as a *'C'* grade student. Then each year I kept on seeing at the same letter for science on all my report cards. Due to repetitively looking at the letter *'C,'* this idea got planted into the garden of my mind (subconscious) which then formed my Self-Image for a school grade. I was automatically programmed to get a *'C'* grade every year because it was in sync with the image I held of myself in my mind. Then suddenly, in the seventh grade, I started thinking positively about school which allowed me to feel better about my grades and that lead to the action of trying new studying habits as I worked harder just before the final exam. This is why I was able to attract the *'A'* grade in physics.

The cybernetic instrument was my Self-Image of a **'C' Grade Student**, and it detected the deviation from the set target of only receiving a *'C'* grade. As soon as it noticed that I studied harder to get a better grade in physics, the cybernetic instrument sent information to my mind which commanded my body to use the old studying habits that I have been doing for years. As a sleepwalker, I never programmed my subconscious to use the new studying habits that got me that *'A'* grade in physics. This is why in the eighth grade, no matter how hard I studied, I continued to receive a *'C'* grade in physics since I never changed my Self-Image for a school grade. If I would have changed the **'C' Grade Student** image in my subconscious mind and replaced that image with a new positive image, then I would have been able to continuously get better grades every year.

Once I learned about Self-Image Psychology and how it works in harmony with the Subconscious Mind, I was about to graduate, so I couldn't really apply it to myself. I then thought of helping my siblings, cousins, and younger friends improve their grades with the power of their minds. I started coaching them and their grades turned out to be better than they imagined because they followed the master strategies that I provided in the most effective manner. I am grateful that I was able to help them but at the same time, I wish I wasn't sleepwalking throughout my years in school because if I were aware of the Self-Image and how it had been directly affecting my grades then my grades in each class would've drastically improved and I would've avoided so much stress! If you are a student who would like to transform your Self-Image for grades in school or delete limited beliefs about your ability to learn then I could be of help. At first, I used to spend an hour with each student and coach them through video calls, but it got to the point where hundreds of students from all around the globe were asking me for help and I didn't have enough time to help everyone individually so I thought of a solution to this problem. I created a video program with modules for each subject. You are welcome to hear what other students have experienced from taking this particular course at the **Y**oung **M**asterminds **I**nsitue of **S**uccess.

If you are dissatisfied with the results you currently have in life, that is a good thing, because feeling *dissatisfied* puts your mind into a creative state. Always remember, dissatisfaction allowed people to use their imagination to *think* in a certain way as this lead to the advancement of electricity and transportation. If people weren't dissatisfied with the candlelight and the train, then there wouldn't be a light bulb and a plane today. If you are grateful for each and every single thing that has happened to you in the past, is happening in the present and is going to happen in the future, then you'll be content with your life and experience inner happiness. Being grateful is the most important concept, but being dissatisfied will help you ***desire*** a better life just like I did. Humans are perpetual beings of increase that have innate desires for growth. Understand that you have and always will have a natural desire to grow in every part of life, whether you're aware of it or not. There are limits your mind unconsciously believes in and you can only outgrow those limitations by changing your self-image as that will affect your behavior. Your self-image is your own conception of the type of person you are. Throughout your life, you have been building your self-image with beliefs about your identity as a human being. Your image was unconsciously formed from your past experiences; successes and failures, humiliations and triumphs. Keep in mind that your self-image determines your reactions to, life, other people, and also the way you interpret people's reactions towards you. It is really fascinating how your mental picture of yourself affects your thoughts, feelings, actions and even your perceived abilities. You are the person you believe yourself to be, and you are consistently going to be 'that' person in everything you do every day.

I believe you want to improve your life intellectually, physically, emotionally, spiritually, financially and socially so that you can become the Master of Your own Mind. The barrier that will hold you back from excelling is an 'image' that was lodged in your subconscious mind at some point in your life. YOU are 100% responsible for changing that 'image,' because if you don't, then it won't allow you to grow into that ideal person you *desire* to become. If you want to improve your relationships, business's sales, grades in school, or even lose weight, understand that it all requires you to change the image you are holding of yourself in your subconscious mind. Once that image has been changed your whole world automatically changes!

ANYTHING that you really want to do is dependent on how YOU see *you*. If you *desire* to understand how you can leverage the Cosmic Force of Powerful Habits to transform from a **Sleepwalker** in a **Mastermind** and re-build your Self-Image in just 3 weeks, then join the VIP list for the upcoming *Master Your Mirror Program* by going on (www.TheYoungMastermind.com/MYM) The key is to replace the old negative image of yourself with a new positive image, and that is the mirror to your success!

Now that you are aware of *The Mirror to Success*, there is one more thing you need to do before you can learn how to eliminate FEAR and replace it with FAITH.

Finish the **Master Action Plan** for this chapter!

Master Action Plan

1. What negative image are you holding in your mind of yourself that you would like to change? Think about all the images and describe them in detail…

2. Now describe the exact opposite of each image that you wish you had in your mind. You must start desiring to build a new positive self-image. You can do this by remembering that every time you look at your reflection, you must imagine yourself to already be the person that you dream of being.

IGNORE what your senses are telling you, and use your imagination to *feel* as if what you are seeing in your reflection is actually REAL.

3. What habits do you currently have that are destroying your chances of becoming even more successful?

List all the things you do on a daily basis that you know are counterproductive to your success.

4. Why do you have those negative habits ingrained in your mind?

How many years ago did these habits start?

Who or what influenced you to start doing what you did?

5. Take a blank piece of paper and make two columns. In the first column on the left side of the page, write down *6 negative habits* that you currently have. In the second column on the right side of the page, for every negative habit, write down a *positive habit* that you ***desire*** to replace the negative one with.

Make a committed decision that you are going to move into ACTION and build these new habits into your world.

Understand that you are going to experience difficulty and you will naturally want to quit this process and go back to the old negative habits but remember Bob Proctor's quote so you can stay motivated to remain consistent and disciplined.

"Discipline is the ability to give yourself a command and then follow it."

Since you want to become a better version of yourself every single day, I believe that you are able to delete all your old negative habits from your life because you ***desire*** to! Whenever you feel demotivated, look in the mirror ask yourself this question:

What is the point of waking up everyday when I'm not trying to even improve MY life by 1%?

Chapter 8

Education as Entertainment

"I believe that the true road to preeminent success in any line is to make yourself master of that line."

-Andrew Carnegie

Can you imagine where the world would be today if they considered the process of learning to be exciting? Education is entertainment, and no matter how ridiculous that sounds, by the end of this chapter, you will realize this truth. After I reached a state of *Conscious Awareness*, I realized that education is infinite. There is no limit to how much information one can learn. All genuine successful people from the past were lifelong learners. If you can't picture yourself studying in school for your whole life, understand that school is not the only place where you could learn. Learning can happen anywhere in the world. My grandparents once told me about Gandhi, the great student of life, who had such a burning **desire** to learn, that he studied under a street lamp at night, irrespective of circumstances. Now we have access to learn anything and everything due to the abundance of technology.

The first time I experienced *Education as Entertainment* was when my mom placed me in a Montessori school. This method of learning is very synced with the nature of a child and allows a child to learn in an aesthetically stimulating environment. Unlike forced learning, in Montessori, the children are expected to make their own conscious decisions like an adult but they are taught in a method conducive to the subconscious mind's potential. Children who are schooled in Montessori masterminds, Waldorf education, or outdoor natural environments, display a higher self-worth, can think out of the box and have a love for learning. I am forever grateful to my mom because of her, I had this phenomenal exposure at a very early stage in my life. Throughout my years of studying in a traditional school system during grades one through twelve, I did not come home with fantastic grades. I could get high marks in a few classes that were meant to be easy, but otherwise, my grades represented that I was an **'average student.'**

My perspective on education changed in my senior year after I took a chemistry class. Throughout the course, I had low grades. This happened mainly because, at that point in my life, I lacked the ***desire*** to study a subject that I couldn't picture myself using later in life. However, when my chemistry teacher assigned a project, I put my mind to work because gathering information and designing a poster required me to use my creativity. When the time came to present the project to the whole class, I was captivated as I had the sufficient self-confidence to speak in front of an audience comfortably. Every time I put in the genuine effort to create a project, I was naturally motivated to present it to the class because I desired the acknowledgment from my teacher and classmates of my hard work. One afternoon my parents were invited to a private meeting to discuss that my grades were overall low and I needed to improve them. The conversation unexpectedly got to a point where I couldn't control the massive smile on my face! I started feeling so accomplished because Mrs. Muhiba told my parents about how she enjoyed listening to me present projects. She said, *"he may not have the best grades in chemistry, but I know he has enough* *confidence to speak in front of hundreds of people."* When I heard those breathtaking words come out of her mouth, I instantly felt like a **'successful student.'** At that very moment, a new positive *Self-Image* was planted in my mind, while the old negative image of a 'C' grade student that I had been holding on to for all those years finally got erased from my subconscious mind. I am forever grateful to her because out of all her hard-working students; she selected me for the **S**cience **D**epartmental **A**ward in front of my entire high school. When I shook the principle's hand to receive it on stage, I acted like I was expecting the award with a smirk on my face, but deep down I was bewildered. I couldn't comprehend why I was even granted this respectable award in the first place. A few days later, I asked Mrs. Muhiba in private what exactly I had done to deserve the honor. She then told me that she saw a strong *'Will-Power'* in me that I may not have seen in myself.

All of this happened around the same time when I started virtual mentorship from Bob Proctor, so I applied a vital lesson I learned on gratitude. I had already begun practicing to have the **M**aster **A**ttitude of **G**ratitude before I received this award, so I went to that same bookstore where I had picked up my dad's birthday gift, and I bought *The Secret: The Power* by Rhonda Byrnes for my chemistry teacher, who to date remains my favorite teacher from high school. If you have a teacher that you admire, or you aspire to emulate someone, understand that you can be like that person. If you *desire* to be somewhere in life, you must find someone who is successful and is already where you want to be, so you can follow their footsteps and master that path to your success. If you want to learn from that person then think of a way where you could help them improve whatever they are doing. While you take out your time to serve them for free, humbly ask for mentorship. Since this is the age of information, mentorship can take place by listening to audios, watching videos, reading books, or even through dreams.

"A mentor is someone who sees more talent and ability within you, than you see in yourself, and helps bring it out of you."

- Bob Proctor

At this stage of my life, I began to dream of the opportunity to learn from Bob Proctor and in a matter of a couple months, my big dream manifested as I got to ask him very important questions in person. I learned that if I wanted to a be rich, I would have to develop an understanding of prosperity and the only way I could do that was by studying successful people. Forbes Magazine has a list of the most successful billionaires, inventors, and visionaries in history up until the twenty-first century. When I took a look at the educational background of all the members on this list, I couldn't stop laughing! Some of them only attended elementary school, others only participated in formal education until the end of middle school, a few of them only went to high school, some didn't even complete it, and a minority of them spent a year in university before deciding to take a different route of education. I am not suggesting that you mimic these behaviors if you desire to be as successful, but I am suggesting that if you look around, you will find that a variety of ways to educate yourself do exist. People often say they were not able to learn because of financial circumstances. The internet is a blessing since there is an abundance of knowledge that is available for FREE. If you seek knowledge, wisdom, or enlightenment, you are bound to find it when you educate yourself about *you*.

The world's perception of education needs to be rejuvenated, and the first perspective, to begin with, is yours! Education can be exciting if you are *willing* to learn how to transform education into any form of entertainment. You don't have to base learning only on information acquired from school; you have the freedom to educate yourself in whatever it is that appeals to your true nature.

You may enjoy learning one subject more than another, but learning the basics such as Math, English, Science, History, and Geography, are essential. These specific areas of study cover the pyramid of life. In my case, I felt like the information that was taught in calculus was irrelevant to what I desired to learn. I wanted to reach the state of financial freedom, so I would never have any financial concerns, but calculus did not teach me how to manage my money or invest in assets to acquire wealth. The crucial point is that, for me to get wealthy, I would need someone qualified to manage my finances. I would need a professional accountant, and in order for him to have become a *'professional,'* he would have needed to acquire education in those subjects like calculus that were relevant to his career path.

For example, if I wanted to travel on the world's fastest jet, I would need the help of a specialized engineer who studied subjects that I never desired to study. This engineer's dream could have been to create the world's fastest jet, but in order for her dream to convert into a physical reality, she would have needed to educate herself in subjects that she considered interesting or entertaining in any way possible. If she had a burning desire to accomplish her goal and live her dream life, then her entire process of studying would be her own form of *entertainment*. Throughout the journey she was aware that studying particular subjects would help reach her worthy ideal, so she embraced the difficulties and persevered only because of her initial desire. If she didn't have a burning desire, then she wouldn't have had the discipline and motivation to create the world's fastest jet.

> *"Formal education will make you a living; self-education will make you a fortune."*
>
> - Jim Rohn

In high school, I was passionate about my theatre and drama classes because I wanted to enhance my level of confidence. At that point, I was not aware of the long-term effects that these classes would have on me, but deep down I had a dream to act and speak on world stages. A year later after graduating from high school, I acted in Saudi Arabia's first ever Commercial Feature Film; *Born A King*. The crazy part of this whole journey is that after I discovered my family's history with the royalty and King Saud, I was selected to play the role of King Saud in the movie when he was young. Around the same time, I also attracted the opportunity to speak on stage for the Bill and Melinda Gates Foundation on the subject of *"Education as Entertainment"* at Misk Global Forum 2017. In retrospect, if I didn't desire to improve my level of confidence then these dreams wouldn't have manifested in the way they did. In order for me to have developed a higher level of confidence, I had to enroll in drama and theater classes even though they were out of my comfort zone. There were many days where I felt extremely uncomfortable, but I was able to persist only because I had the ***desire***. If I didn't have a desire then I most likely would have skipped more classes and wasted my time. In my last year of high school, I started establishing different methods to *educate* myself that I felt were like *entertainment*, and I still consider them fun, productive activities. I read books that made me aware of my mind's potential and watched videos that showed me how to become more successful than I already was. I listened to audios that taught me how to meditate and I also *learned* how to reprogram my subconscious mind by falling asleep to hypnosis. Furthermore, I got interested in lucid dreaming, but in order for me to experience this form of dreaming, I had to *educate* myself on this subject, which was another version of my *Education as Entertainment*. I began transforming vehicles into moving classrooms by playing audios on success whenever I was in a car, on a plane or even a boat. In my perspective, a moving classroom is not a 'boring' way of learning; rather it is an *'entertaining'* way of learning. If you've never listened to a beneficial audio, then I challenge you to transform any vehicle into a moving classroom! This is exactly how I was able to successfully transform my *education* into my form of *entertainment* and live my dream life. I know for a fact that you can experience this as well because I'm living proof.

Have YOU ever considered the education in school to be entertaining? Most people's answer would be along the lines of: **"no...not really, umm..maybe..? what do you even mean? nope..never are you serious!"** Sadly, there is a minority of people on planet earth who would answer with **"oh yes..for sure, I love learning, I enjoy what I study, understanding new things in life is cool"**

The root cause of this problem stems back to how children were educated from the very early stages of their lives. There is an enormous difference between what people know and what they do and the traditional educational system is responsible for producing humans who have trouble filling in the gap between what they know and what they do. The common person knows how to do their job better but their behavior presents that they don't know any better and they frequently do not do what they already know how to do!

Why do you think most people know so much, but do so less? If you went through formal education, you were unconsciously programmed from day one to gather information in your conscious mind. Then periodically, throughout the school year, you were given a quiz, a test or an exam. When the time came, you were expected to study a book and most likely memorize the content. You then had to answer questions within minutes from whatever you 'studied', and if you answered them correctly you passed, if you answered them incorrectly you failed. Over the years if you passed enough tests or exams, you received a mark and were granted a diploma or degree. The main problem with this system is that it does not genuinely teach you how to *learn* rather it teaches you how to *gather information.* Most people have convinced themselves to believe that gathering information is the real way of learning. In 1970, the futurist Alvin Toffler wrote, "The illiterate of the 21st century will not be those who cannot read and write, but those who cannot learn, unlearn and relearn." His prediction was very accurate as most people nowadays are sleepwalking in a state of ignorance. The process of learning and gathering information both take place in traditional systems, but most schools provide valuable knowledge to these two categories of students. The first category of students study required information because they **desire** to prove they know something. After a period of time, these students end up forgetting a majority of the information that was gathered because the process of *'knowing'* takes place in their conscious mind. However, the second category of students study required information because they **desire** to learn for their own benefit. After a period of time, they are able to teach what they understood to others because the process of *'understanding'* takes place in their subconscious mind. These students who experience genuine learning are only able to because the process education is their own form of entertainment.

> *"In times of change, the learners will inherit the earth; while the learned find themselves beautifully equipped to deal with a world that no longer exists."*
>
> - Eric Hoffer

If you want to be a part of the learners, you need a certain level of balanced confidence. If you have too much confidence you'll think you know everything and if you have too less confidence you won't feel worthy enough to learn anything. Just be willing to learn with a *desire* to expand your level of awareness. There are people that graduate top of their class from the best schools in the world but they are not living the way they really want to live, not earning the money they want to earn, not doing what they love, and most shockingly not working in the field they spent all those years studying for. The reason these people aren't able to attract the results they want in life, even though they have gathered information for years, is because all the valuable knowledge that school provided was stored on their conscious level of mind and not their subconscious level. Most often, these people continue to sleepwalk through life in their comfort zones, settle for average results, remain satisfied and give up on their dreams all because they have lost a *desire*. If YOU cannot imagine your own life to turn out like this, then all you have to do is establish a burning *desire* because without a desire there is no motivation. Once you have a desire, you will naturally be **willing** to study or read something more than once and internalize the content. This will allow your mind to get emotionally involved with what you are studying. If your desire is strong then you will be disciplined enough to get involved in the repetition of educating yourself with information that entertains you. This is how your subconscious mind develops a deeper *understanding* which will lead to genuine learning. This is exactly how **Y**oung **M**asterminds all over the world *learn*.

    The most important factor to remember is that your body is just an instrument of your mind. The subconscious mind is in control of commanding your body to move into action and it's your actions that produce the results you attract into your life. If you want your knowledge to reflect your results, you must first learn how to *think* in a certain way. There are several factors that must be taught and implemented in order to close the gap between what you know and what you do, but it all starts with the act of thinking. In chapter 10, **Serene Thinking**, the solution to this massive problem will be explained.

Did you know there is a huge difference between having an abundance of knowledge and being *educated*? The difference will become obvious if you look up the Latin root from which the word *educate* is originated. The word **'educate'** comes from the Latin word **'educare'**, which means to draw out, to develop from within, to grow through use. It does NOT mean to simply gather information and store knowledge! As you are now a student of life on the journey to become the Master of Your own Mind, you already desire to be a lifelong learner, but most students don't desire lifelong learning. This is because their natural love for learning depletes after many years of formal education due to the method of instruction and the impression a school graduation places on a student's subconscious mind. There is no such thing as an educated person on planet earth because knowledge is infinite. There are students who have acquired a specialized degree, a specific title or a high ranking career position with a big paycheck that believe they are **'educated'** and they no longer need to learn because society confirmed they have gathered more than enough information for years. In 1937, Napoleon Hill concluded, "An educated person is not, necessarily, one who has an abundance of general or specialized knowledge. An educated person is one who has so developed the faculties of the mind that he may acquire anything he wants, or its equivalent, without violating the rights of others." In the next chapter, you will become aware of the faculties he is referring to. Once people develop their mental faculties, they are considered **'educated'** humans.

I have summarized the main issues that traditional educational systems have in regards to sharing knowledge up until this point of the chapter, now I *desire* to only focus on the rejuvenation of education by sharing sustainable solutions with you. The idea of 'learning' should NEVER come off as 'boring' to a child, rather it should stir emotions of excitement and cause the child to *desire* to learn. Due to rapid growth in technology, there are many new forms of entertainment that spark irresistible feelings of attraction within a child's mind, such as the realm of Virtual Reality. At this moment, I want you to stop reading for a second and close your eyes. IMAGINE educating a child's subconscious mind while the child's conscious mind is being entertained. Before I elaborate any further on this vision, I want to ask you a simple question about your childhood.

Did you ever watch a cartoon, tv series or movie on the famous networks of Disney, Nickelodeon, PBS or Cartoon Network?In my first five years of life on earth, I rarely watched television as a kid because for some strange reason my parents never thought of purchasing a TV. The only time I could watch Spiderman and play Super Nintendo was whenever I visited my grandparents because for some strange reason they had video games! Now that I have reached a higher level of awareness in life, I AM forever grateful that my parents didn't own a TV when I was a child.

If YOU were entertained at a young age by television, there is a 99.9% of a chance that you were exposed to numerous subliminal messages without ever realizing it. There are several reports online with visual proof on how content from the world's most famous cartoons, tv series, and films have been using these channels of entertainment to impress nasty, cruel, and self-destructive ideas on billions of people's minds'. Whenever your eyes view a screen, watch something in VR or even observe a hologram, your brainwave cycles eventually slow down until you reach the Aphla level of mind. This is why people naturally start feeling sleepy after staring at a screen for long period of time. When your mind reaches this state after some time of relaxation, subliminal hypnosis can easily start programming your mind without your permission. Understand that subliminal information is a message that goes through your senses and enters your subconscious mind so fast that you don't even hear, see, smell, taste or touch it. The message could help or harm you but regardless, it gets planted into the garden of your mind. So when your brain reaches the Alpha state, any type of negative idea can slip into your subconscious mind and you cannot even stop it because your conscious mind is drowsy as its programmed by the media to be submissive and remain unaware while accepting information. There are researchers at the University of Pennsylvania School of Medicine who estimated that the human retina can transmit visual input at roughly 10 million bits per second! Another research conducted in Berlin calculated that the subconscious mind processes more than 400 billion bits of information per second. That means when you are reading a book, using your phone, watching videos, talking to someone, listening to the radio or doing ANY activity throughout your 24 hours, your subconscious mind is automatically picking up at least 400 billion bits of information every single second without you being fully aware what information your mind is picking up at any moment. This should scare you but excite you at the same time because you are now aware of how much infinite potential you have access to that is naturally being used every day! You can be dominant and leverage your subconscious mind's power to make *life* happen for you or you can be submissive and let media leverage your subconscious mind's power to make life happen to you.

One of my clients is a software engineer and mother of two children. I am forever grateful to her for sharing this phenomenal story with me about her seven year old and four year old kids, because it inspired me to take on this challenge. She explained how her kids watch YouTube videos in their spare time and gain so much scientific knowledge along with *learning* communication and social skills. When I first heard that, I couldn't believe it because I never thought that a cartoon would be able to leave a positive impact on a child's mind, but everything started to make sense as she continued with the story. After her kids watch fun beneficial videos, they share what they learned with their mom as she is always mindblown by their level of awareness at such a young age! While her kids watch the videos, they get emotionally attached to the content as it entertains their subconscious mind and at the same time their minds develop a deeper *understanding*. If they were to just watch the videos without connecting on an emotional level, their minds would just *gather information* for a period of time. The most important factor is that a child's subconscious mind can be *learning* while the conscious mind is being entertained. This is possible because when a child is watching a cartoon, the mind's conscious attention is directed towards understanding the information on the screen at first and then after sometime, the conscious attention slows down as it reaches the Alpha state. Throughout this entire process, the mind's subconscious attention is constantly picking up bits of information. This proves that while a child's conscious mind is entertaining itself, the child's subconscious mind can easily be educating itself without the child needing to be aware that *learning* is taking place.

In conclusion, her children are not much different from any other child on planet earth. These kids just love having fun so they use the media to entertain themselves but at the same time, their minds' are being educated without them fully acknowledging that they have successfully transformed entertainment into their own form of education. The media has been aware of the power to re-program and condition the human mind through different channels of entertainment for centuries. Unfortunately, the media has and is using this power to create subliminal messages that fit their own agenda. However, if cartoons put out positive subliminal messages such as: *learning is so much fun, always feel grateful, broccoli is yummy, fresh juice gives you superpowers, be calm, help others, love yourself, be a giver- not a getter, treat everyone equally, respect elders, invest in yourself, believe in your BIG dreams, exercising is energizing, imagine a better life, only do what you love in life*, then humanity is bound to inevitably prosper because children's minds would be cleansed from the unnecessary garbage.

There is an infinite power of energy always flowing to and through every human being in this universe and the subconscious mind is able to tap into this energy with its mental faculties. Every day this power is either used to serve or destroy humanity. This power can also be used to rejuvenate education only if there is a burning *desire* to render this valuable form of service. If someone puts these phenomenal ideas to ACTION and creates positive content that can serve humanity to such a large extent that future progenies would benefit, then billions of people's minds' would be re-programmed to experience genuine happiness, lifelong health, true love, serenity, with an abundance of wealth. Thanks to the remarkable efforts of Saudi Arabia's Crown Prince Mohammed bin Salman, the entire world's perception of education is being flipped to the idea of ***Education as Entertainment***. International schools, reputed colleges, and universities are adapting to this reality because they are all aware of the fact that change is inevitable but investing in our personal development programs is a profitable choice for every student's mind.

Did you know when I wrote this chapter, the idea of *Education as Entertainment* was just a vision, but now it's an actual documentary on its way to serve billions of human in every nation?! The main thesis *Education as Entertainment* is based on establishing a *desire* to be successful in any area of life. In order to become a success, one must educate themselves in whichever area of study that appeals to them. As long as there is a burning desire to learn, the process of 'education' naturally evolves into the feeling of 'entertainment' because the individual wants to expand their level of awareness to develop a deeper understanding so they can reach their desired destination in life and be even more successful than they already are. Earl Nightingale, the father of the personal development industry, defined 'success' in a profound way.

> *"Success is the progressive realization*
> *of a worthy ideal."*

When you have a definite goal in mind that you desire to accomplish and you have made a committed decision that you are going to get to where you want to go no matter what, then at that very moment, you immediately transform yourself into what is known as a 'successful person'. This is why **Y**oung **M**asterminds always have and always will be known as 'successful people', because they desire to learn forever! After reaching a higher level of *Conscious Awareness*, I realized that most people are successful in their own unique way since they naturally transform education into their own form of entertainment. Let me share my perspective so you can realize that you are as well.

Every human is the highest form of creation as they are born with a mind that has infinite potential power. The majority of humans love entertaining their mind because it makes them *feel* better. The human mind is able to feel amazing due to the energy in that particular form of entertainment resonates with the emotional part of the human mind; Subconscious. This is why billions of humans all over the planet love entertaining themselves through sports, music, movies and video games. If these forms of entertainment didn't evoke a strong *feeling* in the subconscious then fans in sports arenas or concerts wouldn't rage and dance, audiences in theatres wouldn't physically get scared while watching a horror movie, and gamers wouldn't lose their temper if they died in the game. Furthermore, while humans entertain their mind, they end up educating their mind at the same time whether they are aware of it or not because they have a ***desire*** to know more. Most humans want to learn more about their favorite character's story, artist's music history or background, and athlete's track record. People who are check gossip news and sports updates only do, because they are curious. When they find out more news they automatically 'educate' their mind on what *feels* to be 'entertainment'. This shows that most humans enjoy consuming information with the purpose to expand their level of awareness in anything since they are attracted to learn more about what they don't fully understand. If this is how the common human behaves, then the solution to education's current problem is very straightforward.

    Before I share the Master Solution in one sentence I would like to explain why I have a burning ***desire*** to solve this challenging world problem. I love spreading light as it diminishes darkness. I'm motivated to render this service because Elon Musk desired to rejuvenate transportation and he did, so I know for a fact that my burning desire to rejuvenate the education is bound to happen whether people like it or not. Education can only be improved when the information that is taught sparks an attraction in the human mind. Bob Proctor once said, "..humans are perpetual beings of increase." This means that YOU have a natural ***desire*** to grow and improve all areas of your life. In order to master your entire life, you must be a Mastermind. I always will be here to guide you on the true path of light that leads to becoming the **Master of Your Own Mind**, through events and programs, but I'm not sure if I would be able to help every single human being on planet earth. This is what YOU can do if you have a child, cousin, sibling, relative or anyone who you can influence. Build the ***desire*** for mastering every part of life in that child's subconscious mind from a young age. You can do this by helping them figure out what they enjoy doing, then show them that if they want to do what they love and earn money so they can live their dream life, all they would have to do is learn what they like.

Eventually, the ***desire*** for experiencing a genuine successful life will naturally cause that person to grow up with the willingness to learn the strange secrets to success while considering the process of *education* to be their own form of *entertainment*.

All successful

Young Masterminds

in history experienced <u>Introspection</u>.

If you are wondering exactly how you can start to do

this, so you can feel the state of introspection,

then I suggest you take as much time

as you need to think and

complete this entire

Master Action Plan

At the end of the day, ***life*** is meant to be fulfilling and purposeful. To experience a meaningful life, you must convert the *education* you need into any form of *entertainment*. YOU will only be able to experience this after you have defined an exact purpose for your life. Always remember, there is not a single soul on earth like you, because YOU are a creative spiritual human being that is unique. That means that your life has a special meaning to it and you will soon discover what you love doing every single day for the rest of your life. If you have already discovered your life's purpose, and you are aware of the worthy ideal that you desire to dedicate your life to accomplish, then the process of ***life*** will be *entertainment* for you.

Now that you are aware of *Education as Entertainment*, there is one more thing you need to do before you can learn Steve Job's secret to success that he used to make billions of dollars!

Finish the **Master Action Plan** for this chapter!

Master Action Plan

1. Spend some time alone and think about what you really want in life. This is your ultimate Dream/Passion/ Desire/Calling in life.

Once you have identified your heart's desire, create a picture with your imagination of exactly how that amazing *'perfect life'* would be if you were living in it right NOW.

Be as specific as you can and explain each and every single thing in deep detail. This page is not long enough, so please take out a notebook and pen or pencil. Start painting the picture that you see in your mind in writing onto paper.

2. Once you feel like you are confident in what you wrote, then ask yourself: "Why do you really want that?"

After deeply thinking of the answer, explain your WHY on a new page in the same notebook. Remember to be fully honest with yourself and go into as much detail as you can to express all your emotions.

3. Dig deeper and try your best to understand what **desire** your soul is really seeking. Are you seeking a particular feeling, a specific person, a new lifestyle, a material object, a past memory?

Think about what will bring your soul fulfillment. Take as long as you want to completely answer these powerful questions and even if it takes you days, weeks or even months to get an answer from your heart, do it!

Once you have thought about everything, then return to your notebook and write down the truth.

4. If you are blessed with the ability to browse the internet, then search for resources that will allow you to *entertain* yourself with the *education* necessary to bridge the gap between your **desire** and your life's purpose.

Make a list of all the things that you really want to learn. If you have a **desire** to learn anything on your list, that means you consider it to be a form of *'entertainment'*.

5. What part of the population do you want to be a part of ? Circle your answer.

Remember that quote:

   a) 2% of the people think

   b) 3% of the people *think* they think

   c) 95% of the people would rather die than think

6. If you have a *desire* to rejuvenate education and would like to work in harmony with my team and me towards fulfilling the higher purpose of diminishing darkness (ignorance) by emitting light (knowledge), then you are welcome to send in an email and share your idea.

Contact details are listed on the last page of this book

Chapter 9

Serene Thinking

"This silence, this moment, every moment, if it's genuinely inside you, brings what you need..."

-Rumi

Do you know someone who seems to always be at peace? Their voice is smooth and relaxing, and they seem compassionate. They never look like in a hurry, and overall they give off positive energy. The person that perfectly fits this description is a successful mastermind. They will always live in abundance because their soul is calm. In today's world, very few people experience *calmness of mind*. What's the point of being calm in such a fast-paced world, you may wonder? If you want to become the Master of Your own Mind, then you must fall in love with the idea of being calm.

There are wealthy people in this world who cannot experience calmness in their lives because they have opted out of seeking a life of inner peace. Although their outer life may appear attractive to the eye, their inner life is nothing but turmoil. You may know some people who have short fuses. They scream at their employees and loved ones, argue on the phone, pick fights for fun, look down on others, and mainly give off negativity energy. Unfortunately, these individuals are living in the dark because they simply aren't aware of **Serene Thinking**. If they *desire* to live in serenity, they would need to seek enlightenment and learn how to *think* in a certain way.

> *"2% of the people think, 3% **think** they think, and 95% would rather die than think!"*
>
> - Dr. Kenneth McFarland

Do you know why the majority of humans don't think? I DARE you to actually take a second to ***think*** why most people don't *think* in a certain way. George Bernard Shaw once said, "Most people think two to three times a year." Bob Proctor told me that he once heard, Earl Nightingale say, "If the average person said what they were thinking they would be speechless." Keep in mind, the act of *thinking* is the most powerful function that YOU are capable of doing as a human, but *thinking* in a certain way is not as simple as it sounds. Henry Ford proclaimed, "Thinking is the hardest work there is, which is probably the reason why so few engage in it." Throughout your day, the thoughts you might have inside your head are usually just internal conversations, projections of the future or experiences from the past. At this moment while you are reading these sentences, there are small thoughts flowing through your mind, but this doesn't mean you're *thinking* in a certain way, scientists would call this 'mental activity'. If you were born on planet earth then you were conditioned to *think* with your five senses. If you think with your senses, then most of the time you let your environment control your thoughts. As you know, thoughts cause feelings, which lead to actions, that create results. So if YOU really want to positively change your life, and become the Master of Your own Mind then you must learn how to *think* in a certain way.

Approximately 90% of the human population allow conditions, circumstances, and environments to control their thinking on a daily basis. The human act of thinking is a skill that can be learned just like how people learn the skill of playing piano or typing. There are a few schools around the world that offer courses which are only devoted to teaching the subject of thinking. The problem is most people don't get the opportunity to attend those schools, rather they are expected to learn and teach thinking as a by-product of studying history, science, language, and math. These subjects do in fact develop thinking in the mind to some extent but the problem is people learn the skill of thinking in bits and pieces and never master the skill. If people were asked how to *think* effectively in a certain way, most wouldn't be able to explain. This is why the common person isn't able to assess their thinking skills or systematically teach the skill of thinking to others. The few institutes around the world that do offer practical courses on thinking all have a similar thesis. Their main thesis is based on the fact that human beings are the only creatures on earth that are able to *think* in a certain way. If that resonates with you, then ask yourself why you've been conditioned to only *think* with your five senses. You may never find out because this way of thinking has been passed down for generations and not many people have questioned this common way of *thinking*. Animals react by instinct, which means they also think with their five senses. So if YOU as a human being are the highest form of creation, then why are you *thinking* in a similar manner?

There must be a secret way to *think* because there are only a few humans who are able to accomplish extraordinary things and experience a phenomenal life. Society labels them as visionaries, philanthropists, inventors, entrepreneurs, and masterminds. The truth is that every 'successful person' is no different than you since they are also a human being who was born with a gold mine between two ears; the human MIND!

Understand, there is a certain way to *think* with your mind and if you want to become a **M**aster **T**hinker then you must start *thinking* with all of your mental faculties. You have six magnificent faculties and they have always existed in the human mind, but not every human is aware of the priceless gifts they were born with. Now you must be wondering what are they..?

The 6 Mental Faculties of a Mastermind

1) Reason

2) Memory

3) Perception

4) Imagination

5) Will

6) Intuition

The world's most successful people from the past, including all prophets, pharaohs, philosophers, scholars, scientists, surgeons, alchemists, idealists, theologians, and missionaries used to *think* with their 6 mental faculties instead of only *thinking* with their 5 senses. Most people in the 21st-century unconsciously use their mental faculties to attract negative results in their own lives in a variety of ways because they weren't taught how to leverage these faculties to unlock their infinite potential. Are you aware that YOU have been using your six mental faculties randomly throughout your life to do different things whether you were aware of it or not? Unfortunately, the media has conditioned people's minds to use their mental faculties in a negative way without even realizing it. For example, when a horrible news reports go viral, billions of people around the world watch the breaking news and start to use their faculty of imagination to envision the worst possible outcome since people are programmed to imagine what they don't want even though it will never benefit them in any way. If people weren't negatively conditioned by society and media, they would use their faculty of imagination to envision the best possible outcome or believe they could get what they want in life!

These faculties are extremely powerful because they are designed in such a way for you to use them to live the 'dream life' you've always desired by working with your inner world. Always remember, there are two worlds that you are working with every day of your life whether you are aware of them or not. The outer world and the inner world. Whenever your mind is *thinking* or *feeling* you are working with your inner world and when your mind commands your body to act upon your *feelings*, an equal or opposite reaction is created and then is presented to you in your outer world. This is why your mental state of mind (inner world) is a reflection of your environment (outer world). If you want to live your dream right now, you must learn how to *think* like a **M**aster **T**hinker. If your environment controls your thought process, this means you were programmed like I was at a young age to use your five senses to *think*. The five senses are important because they help you accomplish your daily tasks, but the six mental faculties are even more important because they help you accomplish your biggest goals. My wildest dreams only manifested when I started to use my six mental faculties to *think* since they allowed me to be in control of my inner world and helped me ignore what my five senses presented in my outer world. This is what **M**aster **T**hinkers do.

After reaching a higher level of *Conscious Awareness*, I know for a fact that if I continued to accept the illusions in my outer world by *thinking* with my five senses, then I wouldn't have accomplished any of my biggest goals! Always remember what Einstein said," The same level of thinking that got you to where you are will not get you to where you want to go."

YOU can easily transform into a Master Thinker, but you must always be in control of your inner world. If you want to *learn* how to use your six higher faculties in the most effective way so you can attract anything into your life within the wink of an eye, then you may inquire more about this elite program to see if you are prepared for **Thinking Mastery**.

> *"An educated person is one*
> *who has so developed the faculties*
> *of the mind that he may acquire anything*
> *he wants, or its equivalent, without*
> *violating the rights of others."*
> -Napolean Hill

In 1903, James Allen published, *As a Man Thinketh*. Below is my commentary on the last chapter from his profound book.

Serenity

"Calmness of mind is one of the beautiful jewels of wisdom."

It requires you to have long and patient effort in the act of self-control. You can only feel complete *'serenity'* in your life after you have developed a more than ordinary knowledge of the universal laws and the way in which your thoughts operate.

You can only become calm if you understand yourself as a thought-evolved being. This knowledge will then allow you to understand others and their way of thinking. When you develop this type of deep understanding on life, you will have a new calm perspective and it will allow you to clearly see how every single thing in your world is related to the action of *cause* and *effect*. Then you will no longer complain and worry, rather you will be able to remain tranquil, devoted, and serene.

Once you become a calm person, you will be able to responsibly manage yourself, and you will know how to adapt yourself to others; and in return, they will feel deep respect for your spiritual strength, and others will feel that they can learn from your association and rely upon you. The more tranquil you become, the greater will be your success, your influence and your power for spreading light. Even if an average person developed *Serene Thinking*, their business's prosperity would increase because that person would have a greater control of themselves and an overall calmness in their life.

Understand that people will always prefer to deal with you if you're behavior is not easily affected by any externalities and if you know how to **Respond** instead of **React** to everything that happens throughout your day.

The strong calm person is always loved and respected. This person is like a palm tree in a thirsty desert or a sheltering rock in a heavy storm.

"Who doesn't love a tranquil heart, a sweet-tempered, balanced life? It does not matter whether it rains or shines, or what changes come to those possessing these calm blessings, for they are always cheerful, serene, and composed. That exquisite balance of character which we call **'serenity'** *is the last lesson of culture; it is the flowering of life, the fruitage of*

the soul."

The *feeling* of a calm mind is as precious as wisdom, and it should be desired more than gold—yup, than even fine gold! How useless does acquiring money look in comparison to living a life full of serenity and joy; a life that resides in the oceans of truth, beneath the waves, beyond the windy storms in the blessings of calmness!

How many people do you know who poison lives, and ruin all that is beautiful about themselves by their explosive tempers? These people end up destroying their balance of character, and make bad blood with others!

Do you think the majority of people ruin their lives and spoil their happiness by a lack of self-control?

There are only a few people that you would come across in life who are well balanced, who have that elegant control which is characteristic of the finished character!

Yes, humanity erupts with undisciplined emotions, humanity is loud with uncontrolled sadness, and humanity is blown away by anxiety and doubt. Only the wise person whose thoughts are controlled and purified makes the winds and the storms of the soul obey them.

Oh calm lost souls, wherever you are, under whatever conditions you may live in, understand this: in the ocean of life the islands of blessedness are smiling, and the sunny shore of your worthy ideal awaits your coming...

Keep your hands firmly on the steering wheel of thought. In the ship of your soul reclines the one and only commanding

Mastermind; He does nothing but sleep, so..WAKE HIM UP!

<u>Self-Control is Strength</u>

<u>Right Thought is Mastery</u>

<u>Calmness is Power</u>

Touch your heart and say:

*"Peace be still, Peace be still, Peace be still,
Peace be still, Peace be still"*

Peace, stillness, serenity, and calmness are all words that may sound similar, but they have deep meanings. *Serene Thinking* is what all genuinely successful people have, and that is why they are able to emit love by tapping into the state of oneness. You must dive deep into the beauty of serenity and the hidden power of being calm to understand how to think in a serene manner. Every time I read the original text of *Serenity*, by James Allen, my level of awareness expands, and I gain deeper insight into its marvelous meaning.

If you want to pursue your dreams and accomplish great things in life, then you must limit yourself from activities that distract you and don't serve your purpose. Deep down you are aware of and responsible enough to acknowledge that you do things throughout your day that may never help in reaching your desired destination or improve your life in any way. If you consciously make a committed decision to stop doing the useless things then you will naturally be disciplined and strong enough to control your ego. If you allow the outside world to control your state, then you are going backward in life because you are reacting. When you react towards a person, to a circumstance or in an environment, you automatically allow it to negatively affect your attitude because it caused you to lose your temper. When I used to be a Sleepwalker, I was a victim of this. Whenever something negative happened to me, I would express my frustration by reacting. I would either annoy my younger brother or sister, punch the wall, kick my bed or use negative swear words. These actions caused me to lose control of myself and my environment. Bob Proctor taught me a fundamental lesson on the subject of responsibility that involved the concept of responding instead of *re-acting*. This lesson is so hard but so important if you want to become the Master of Your Own Mind.

If someone shouts in your presence, and without even thinking, you quickly shout back in anger, you automatically become a sleepwalker. This is because you have lost control of yourself since you *reacted*. On the other hand, if someone shouts in your presence and you take a second to THINK, and then you decide to *respond* back to that person, you automatically become a Mastermind. This is because you were in control of yourself. Every time something happens in your life before you do anything, remember this:

If you choose to **React**, you immediately move backward in life and stay in a Sleepwalker frequency, but if you choose to **Respond**, you automatically move forward in life and vibrate on the frequency of a Mastermind.

Have you ever tried meditation? If you didn't then that's amazing, but if you did, thats also amazing. See nothing is good or bad, it's just our thinking perspective that makes it so. Everything in this universe just is. Nature is a perfect example because if you take a deeper look into nature it just is the way it is. Nature is always meditating, it's just your level of awareness that will either allow you to recognize this truth or not. The idea of meditating became famous in the 21st century but the practice of it has existed from the beginning of time. The most successful people from every era of history were masters of meditation. When they became aware of meditation's life-altering benefits, they chose to learn the art of meditation. Understand that everyone meditates throughout their day in their own way, but not everyone is consciously aware of what they are doing with their mind, body, and soul. The act of meditation naturally takes place either consciously or unconsciously. I started consciously meditating at the age of 18, but before that, I had been unconsciously meditating for years as I was sleepwalking. Once my soul reached a higher level of *Conscious Awareness*, I understood the infinite benefits of engaging in meditation on a daily basis. The day I found out that meditation could increase the abundance I attract into my life, I got so excited that I wanted to apply everything that I learned. Starting off with guided meditation was the best option for me. Guided meditation persuades the mind to slow down which allows the mind to command the body to relax. It didn't take that long until I found my favorite meditation to listen to. Throughout this journey, I stayed consistent with listening to the exact same audio every single morning until it became a master habit. There were times when I got to meditate on the roof of my house, in a kayak on the lake, in the clouds on a plane, on the middle of a highway in the car, on a train, in hot tubs, on sandy beaches, in the middle of a forest and desert, under a waterfall, on the peak of a mountain, laying down on grass and even in saunas!

The meditation track I listened to for over a year was on the subject of ABUNDANCE and because I allowed my mind to get repetitive exposure to the sound, my subconscious mind got programmed to notice abundance in every single thing. One thing led to another and my life was full of even more abundance. At the time I didn't know what I was doing but later I realized that it was because I re-programmed my mind to only focus on abundance and that is all I attracted into my life since where focus goes, energy flows. I got so emotionally connected to meditating as it made me *feel* better than ever that I began to practice it religiously five times a day! Once meditation became a part of me, I was able to experience *Serene Thinking*.

If you really want to experience *Serene Thinking*, then all you have to do is hold on to your burning desire and never let it vanish. You may desire to think in a serene manner is because your soul enjoys the feeling of calmness since it's harmless. Meditation's purpose is to show you what is already yours, to bring meaning to your life and to uncover who you really are. If you have a massive problem, and you are confused, *Serene Thinking* will allow you to identify the exact problem as the solution will naturally present itself to you. During meditation, *Serene Thinking* helps eliminate any worries in your outer world and guides your mind to exploring the undiscovered inner world that is yours!

The monks, yogis, masterminds, prophets, and gurus were all humans who fell in love with the feeling of meditation. They experienced *Serene Thinking* on a consistent basis (247/365) since they went to war with their ego. There were very successful human beings who have left a deep impact on this planet and since their routine revolved around meditation. There are still humans in the 21st century who are able to leave a deep positive impact on billions of lives. Steve Jobs is a great example. Some hate him and some love him but at the end of the day, he left a deep impact on planet earth. The only reason he was worth billions was because he served billions of people through his products and services. In **Chapter 10: Money 101**, you will learn how important rendering service is. Jobs experienced *Serene Thinking* because he was searching for higher truths to life. He was known as the entrepreneur who meditated in Japan. Meditation allowed him to identify his burning desire and express it through the creation of Mac, which led to the creation of many other devices. A piece of software transformed into a personal computer that allows countless millions of humans to tap into a creative state and produce beautiful content. I am forever grateful to Jobs for using his imagination because the MacBook I am typing from right now allows me to express my creativity in phenomenal ways. Everything I do successfully is produced from this extraordinary machine. It's interesting how this Macbook was once a crazy idea but now it is a hard fact. The success formula of *Serene Thinking* allowed Steve Jobs to meditate like an **A**bundant **M**astermind, live for his worthy ideal and manifest his life's desires which ended up serving humanity in marvelous ways!

You can essentially become a Mind Architect like Steve Jobs, and create a Master Design of the calm life you would love to live. Look around you right now and realize that every material object was only created when someone used their mind to identify their desire, then made the desire a goal, imagined what they wanted, eliminated all fear, and persistently worked at making it a physical reality. To experience the peace of *Serene Thinking*, you can start with learning how to meditate effectively like an **A**bundant **M**astermind. Many people have learned how to attract abundance after listening to the ***Abundant Mastermind Meditation***. The most effective methods that you may adopt in order to develop serenity in life are guided meditations, peaceful associations, and environments that have a connection with nature.

Now that you are aware of *Serene Thinking*, there is one more thing you need to do before you can learn the Master Money Strategy that 1% of the world use to generate infinite wealth.

Finish the **Master Action Plan** for this chapter!

Master Action Plan

1. List as many things in your life that are not allowing you to experience a calm peaceful life?

-
-
-
-
-
-
-
-
-
-
-
-
-
-
-

2. Did you ever experience *Serene Thinking*? If so, recall how it felt, what time of the day it happened, and what environment did you surround yourself in. If you feel like you never experienced *Serene Thinking*, then I recommend you start with guided meditation.

3. Think of someone in your life who brings you nothing but **chaos**. List 5 things about this person that causes you to *feel* negative. Now, think of someone who brings the opposite effect; **calmness**. List 5 things about this person that causes you to *feel* positive. List any desirable traits this calm person has that you wish to embody?

Chaos

1.

2.

3.

4.

5.

Calmness

1.

2.

3.

4.

5.

4. After reading this chapter, you should be aware of the fact that ***'Thoughts are Things'***.

Think about a time when you attracted something in your life just by <u>thinking</u> a <u>thought</u>. This could be a positive thought which created a positive outcome or a negative thought which created a negative outcome. Once you are done *thinking* about this, write a short summary of what happened below.

5. The six higher faculties that you have in your subconscious mind were created to help you control your inner world so you can create your dream life in your outer world. What are the names of each faculty?

1)

2)

3)

4)

5)

6)

If you cannot remember all the names, then you should understand what these faculties are, how they operate in your subconscious mind and how you can make all six of them work for you within the wink of an eye!

6. If you are curious how *life* is like for people who transformed into **A**bundant **M**asterminds, then try listening to the ***Abundant Mastermind Meditation***. There is a bonus guided meditation audio thats waiting for YOU in this video & audio program!

Go to: TheYoungMastermind.com/Meditation

Chapter 10

Money 101

"Knowledge is better than wealth, because knowledge protects you while you protect wealth."

-Ali

Are you willing to dedicate your entire life to work for money? After reading Robert Kiyosaki's *Rich Dad Poor Dad*, I made the decision to never work for money, rather make money work for me. Although I was born rich with a gold mine between my ears, like yourself, I always desired to live a happy, healthy, and wealthy life. Bob Proctor taught me that not everybody wants to be wealthy, but everyone wants to be free from any financial concerns. When Bob read the first version my book, he knew I desired to be a very wealthy person and I heard him say, *"The real reason you want to get rich is because...you want to be able to extend the service that you offer far beyond your own presence."* I realized that his intuition picked up my heart's burning desire. I don't want to be wealthy to fulfill my ego; rather I want to be wealthy, so I have an abundance of time to do what I love without ever having any financial concerns.

I ***desire*** to genuinely help every single nation by bringing people into a state of *Conscious Awareness* of their infinite potential because this is my worthy ideal. At the age of 19, I realized that my mission in life is to show 1 billion human beings how to become Young MasterMinds!

Did you ever wonder how rich people become wealthy and how they are able to continuously attract an abundance of ever-flowing prosperity into their lives? You may have heard of these types of people, and their lifestyle may blow your mind to some extent, but in their perception it's a 'normal' way of living. IMAGINE entering your favorite store and buying all the things you want without ever having to worry about looking at the price tag. Imagine being able to book a first-class flight to wherever you want to go, without asking yourself if you have time to go on vacation. Imagine having so much time on your hands that you can spend it doing the things you love with your family. Imagine you never had to work a job, and instead, you were able to earn money around the clock without the need to be somewhere for a given period of time. If you can even slightly picture yourself living a life where you have an abundance of time and money freedom, I guarantee you that it is 100% POSSIBLE.

Remember if YOU can see what you want in your mind's eye then you can see it with your actual eyes! Only a minority of people can really live extraordinary lives because their lives are full of this freedom. Some people hate this minority, and some people idolize this minority. They might be the one percent who continue getting richer, but there is a reason why they keep attracting riches into their life. They think, feel and act differently which is exactly why they experience *life* differently. Do you know exactly what this minority of human beings do differently? If you want to live life on your own terms and reach the state of financial freedom, then you must learn how to generate wealth. In Bob Proctor's *MATRIXx* event, he mentioned exactly how successful people in history generated wealth and how only a few people still know the master secret to attracting riches throughout life without any abundance blocks. This is what I learned about earning money.

Let's start with Master Money Strategy One (M²S1). This strategy involves trading time for money. Approximately 96% of the population is trade their time for money. Unfortunately, this strategy that people are conditioned to use is not able to generate long-term wealth because of saturation. Time is the most limited asset you have, so to earn more money, you must work for more hours. The problem is you only have **24** hours in a day, which means there is a limit to how much money you can earn. In most industries, the common professions and jobs require you to trade your most limited asset; time for money. The people who got rich trading their time for money were only able to generate wealth at the expense of a lifetime. These people had to compromise the car they drove, the vacations they took, the home and schooling they provided for their kids, and the clothes they wore because they needed enough money to meet all of their expenses. This is a never-ending story of the rat race! If you want to be a part of mediocrity, go ahead.

Master Money Strategy Two, (M²S2) is only used by 2-3% of the population. This is when people invest money to generate a return on investment. This is a very powerful strategy, but only people who really take out the time to learn it, are able to benefit from it. There are only three out of 100 people who understand that leverage is a great way to make this strategy work for you. The most successful person I know who mastered this strategy is HRH Prince Alwaleed Bin Talal, known as the *Arabian Warren Buffet*. If you want to master this strategy, learn from someone who has established an authority on investing and their results prove they know what they are talking about, then do exactly as they say.

Master Money Strategy Three (M2S3) is only used by 1% of

the population and this minority is earning 96% off all the money that's being earned. This master strategy allows you to have an abundance of time and money freedom. Approximately only one percent of the population use this strategy, and they have multiple streams of income. There is not a single wealthy person in history who generated wealth from only one source; wealth generation requires multiple sources. If you want to master this strategy, you need to start multiplying your time through the efforts of others, and this will allow you to set up multiple streams of income. Always remember another source of income doesn't mean a second job. The most efficient way to open another source of income is to direct your focus on creating passive income.

The most common examples for opening up passive sources of income:

- rent your mailing list for a fee
- real estate investing
- franchise something
- intellectual property (give your idea to someone else to take to market and receive a royalty)
- write a book, song, play, or movie script
- publish a book that is available under public domain
- invent something
- backend sales (real estate agents use for referrals)
- facilitate/market something for someone else get an insurance or securities license (residual income)
- web based affiliate programs (they're all over the place)

These are just a few ways to multiply your time through the efforts of others so you can generate multiple sources of income, but you can always use your imagination to come up with your own ways as there are no limits since the universe is the infinite source of supply! Keep in mind, a passive source of income means it shouldn't take a lot of your time or energy...it's just something that's there, where you receive money on a regular basis because you have contributed in some way or another. Granted, there may be an initial output of time and energy to get it rolling, but after that start-up phase, it's considered 'earning money while you sleep'. If you make the decision to learn how to use (M^2S^3), then eventually money will be working for you. This will give you the opportunity to have all the time you need to do whatever your soul desires.

Did you know there is a Universal Law that controls how much money you can earn? It's called the **Law of Compensation**. This law clearly states the amount of money you earn in life will always be in exact ratio to the demand for what you do, your ability to do it and the difficulty there will be in replacing you. All you need to focus on is your ability to do what you do. If you try to improve your quality of service every day and get better at doing it then you can earn as much money as you desire. Aim to be a Master at whatever you do in life and maintain a sense of urgency. If you get a lot of work done in a short period of time in a calm and confident manner then you will naturally develop a sense of urgency. One major factor that distinguishes people who make things happen from those who don't is the way they do their work each day. I used to be like most people who are always busy but rarely accomplish anything. I learned that people who make things happen are focused on a specific target. They know where they're going and what they need to do to get there. They have intensity, a focal point, a purpose. Masterminds work with a sense of urgency, they get a lot done in a short period of time. When you work with a sense of urgency, you're thinking 10 times bigger than everyone else. You' don't have to work harder, you just work more efficiently through systematic thought instead of random action. Learn to make your work count by developing a definite purpose of what you want to do along with a Master Action Plan to achieve it. In so doing, you'll no longer work like a Sleepwalker.

I learned a lot about life and success from Mr. Earl Nightingale. In the year 1987, he published a recording on the master truth behind money. You won't ever find a class in a traditional school, college, or university that strictly only focuses on the subject of money, but you may find a masterclass in the near future at the **Y**oung **M**asterminds **I**nstitute of **S**uccess that only focuses on the subject of money and the generation of multiple streams of income...

Are you ready to attend
Master class-
Money 101?

Below is a summarized excerpt from Earl Nightingale's *"Let's Talk About Money"* audio record.

Money is not bad. Money is important. Money is only used for two things. To live a comfortable life without any financial stress and to extend the service you provide beyond your physical presense. Money is the harvest of your production. The more money you can count, the more you can produce. Money doesn't buy happiness; however, it buys a lot more happiness than poverty. Many of the good things in life are only possible to experience with money. Money is the only reward that is completely negotiable and can be used by everyone. The amount of money you receive in life regardless of what you do is always in direct proportion to these three things.

- The demand for what you do
- Your ability to do the work you do
- The difficulty there is in replacing you

Your ability to see opportunities depends on how well you have prepared yourself for accumulating riches. If you want more money, then take out time to qualify yourself for it. The world will pay you exactly what you bargain for, your skills or gifts. Your rewards will always be in exact proportion to your service. If you want to increase your income, you can only do it by increasing your value. If you want to learn how to attract money into your life, you must first decide how much money you really want. Most people never decide how much money they want to earn, save, or put aside for future retirement. There are only three amounts of money every single human being should decide upon. Firstly, the exact amount of money you want to earn yearly, now or in the near future. Secondly, the exact amount of money you want to have as a life's savings that could be used for investment. Lastly, the exact amount of money you want to have as retirement income, whether you retire from your active work or not.

Most people make a very serious mistake; they never decide on any one of these three amounts of money. If you make these three important decisions and write them on a card to carry with you or put someplace where you can review it from time to time, you will automatically have placed yourself in the top five percent of the people.

You will have a plan for your future and a blueprint for your financial accomplishment; you will know where you are going, and if you are serious about it, you will most certainly get to your desired destination. Sleepwalkers don't have trouble in achieving their goals; they can do that. They have trouble setting extraordinary goals; they leave their life to chance and find out sooner or later that chance doesn't work, and they have missed the boat. It's estimated only five percent of people decide on the money they will earn and then grow as individuals into the size of the incomes they seek. These masterminds are able to take their lives, fortunes, and futures into their own hands as they should and accomplish their goals right on schedule every year! You can do the same thing. You can do it starting right now!

Understand these principles, and they will bring you everything you want: it is not the job, it is the person, and it's not your present circumstances that count, but the circumstances you make up your mind to achieve that is important. The only limit on your income is YOU, and the income you decide upon can be achieved within the framework of your present work, industry, or profession where you already have a start and a place. All you need is a plan, the roadmap, and the courage to press on to your destination, knowing in advance many problems will arise, and setbacks will occur. Remember, nothing on earth can stand in the way of a plan backed by faith, purposeful persistence and determination. By setting a financial goal, you're demonstrating faith, and you will find that you will begin to become what others call *'lucky.'* You will soon discover that you are no longer the same person. Believe in yourself to such an extent that you can feel and the quiet inner voice that has faith you **will** accomplish all your goals.

At the end of the day, realize that money cannot be attracted directly, money like happiness is an effect as a result of a cause, and the cause is valuable service. Keep money in its proper place. It is a **Servant**, nothing more. You are the **Master**. It is a tool to use to live a better life. Too much emphasis on money reverses the whole picture, and you become the **Servant**, and money becomes the **Master**. It is nice to have money and the things money can buy, but it's good to check up once in a while and make sure that you haven't lost the things money can't buy that is, friends and family.

Master's Insight

"What money? Paper money. Paper is not money. Excuse us! This is paper, gold is precious. Do you use gold in the toilet!? They have forgotten that they are human beings."

– Mohammed Adil

THE WORLD IS CHANGING and even though paper money is the dominant medium of exchange for goods and services used in the 21st century, it's value is slowly dissipating due to the creation of cryptocurrencies and advancements in digitalization. The chapter on Self-Image illustrates the importance of holding a valuable image of yourself in your mind. Since YOU are the highest form of creation; any compensation you earn in return for the service you render should be according to your exalted status. The highest and most valuable form of monetary compensation is gold. If you want to feel excited about attracting riches, then imagine your wealth in ounces of gold as opposed to other forms of currency, which can suddenly lose value or even be easily counterfeited. You can do this by deciding upon the amount you of gold you desire to have for yearly income, savings, and future retirement. This concept will resonate with people who desire to generate massive amounts of wealth since gold is a smart investment in the long run due to the fact that it's a natural resource full of infinite abundance.

The final principle I would like to share with you is very

simple, but it is the most valuable concept you will ever learn about the subject of money. If you want to keep the riches you have attracted in life and never have any financial concerns for the rest of your life, then you must remember that money is just a tool. Do not fall in love with a tool, especially paper. You cannot fall in love with money because if you do, you will unconsciously end up reversing the equation like the men in the following example did. In 1923, eight men were the world's wealthiest financiers. They controlled more money than the United States government at that time. Most people would assume that these individuals were masterminds who lived in abundance, but they were sleepwalkers who lived in ignorance.

Fast forward 25 years later, 3 men committed suicide, the other 3 died in horrible situations, 1 of them went completely insane, and the last man died bankrupt. Their lives got destroyed because after they fell in *love* with money, they started to *use* people to attain it by any means necessary. When you begin using people, your mind starts developing an obsessive love for money. This causes the abundance to stop as the equation is flipped. You become money's **Servant**, and money becomes your **Master**.

The Universal Law of Cause and Effect states, that whatever you do to others, you are really doing to yourself because the universe naturally attracts whatever you send out back into your life regardless whether it was negative or positive. This is why big drug cartels and other illegal businesses eventually die out in some way. The 'cause' would be putting out negativity in any form through products or services, and the 'effect' would be attracting that negativity back into the business as it is bound to happen. There is no way *energy* can be stopped since every single thing happens in an orderly way by Law. If you want to avoid this **Master Money Trap**, so you can always live a life of abundance, then do this from now on with pure intentions. If you make this a habit, you will never end up like any of those eight men.

<u>Reverse the equation:</u> ***use*** money and ***love*** people. A genuine connection with a fellow human is much more valuable than holding on to pieces of paper, storing digital currency, or even polishing gold bars!

In David Schwartz's book, *The Magic of Thinking Big*, he said, "You can't harvest money unless you plant the seeds that grow money. And the seed of money is service. Put service first, and money takes care of itself." I once heard Bob Proctor say something along the lines of, "..you don't go to work to earn money, working is the worst way to earn money, you go to work for satisfaction. You provide service to earn money and you can provide more service in more areas if you will THINK.." When I first heard him say that I was shocked and I thought he was crazy, but after I did some deep *thinking*, it began to make sense. The real reason people work is to gain a *feeling* of fulfillment for their efforts and the real way to earn money is to provide valuable service.

If you want to always earn with abundance, then be a giver by adding more value to your service than the money you receive in return. This may sound crazy to you, but this is one of the most powerful wealth attraction secrets that masterminds use. It's really that simple, but not many people understand this truth to money, as they choose to sleepwalk in ignorance.

If YOU have a financial problem, here is the master solution. Start by *thinking* of any way where you can help at least one person. Identify a common problem that most people have and use your imagination to THINK of any type of solution. The solution doesn't need to change the world, it just needs to be of help. It can be a big or small solution. At first, test your solution on a few people, once it works and you see results, choose a specific target market that you want to focus on helping. Create a small product or service that can help someone and offer it to people for FREE.

Once you have developed trust with your clients or customers, you can start charging many people. Always remember, to sell people on the idea of buying your offer because of how valuable your product or service really is. Keep in mind, your product or service needs to be seen by the people you want to help, so there are many efficient and effective ways to market online, but it all starts with a *desire* and the willingness to *learn*; if you want to earn.

Now that you are aware of *Money 101*, there is one more thing you need to do before you can learn about your 7 levels of Awareness that all Young Masterminds are aware of.

Finish the **Master Action Plan** for this chapter!

Master Action Plan

1. Make a long list all of the negative ideas and beliefs that you once had about money.

2. Do you genuinely BELIEVE that you can be part of the top 5% or 1% of successful people who live a happy, healthy and wealthy life with an abundance of time & money freedom?

If you do, then explain why you *feel* like you will be as successful as you desire to be?

3. Did you listen to Earl Nightingale's advice and answer the three most important questions that predict your Future Financial Fortune? If not, please answer them right NOW in the space provided below.

    1) What is the exact amount of money you want to earn yearly, now or in the future?

    2) What is the exact amount of money you want to have in a savings account?

    3) What is the exact amount of money you want as retirement income?

4. Which form of riches excites you more…attracting paper money or gold bars? If gold excites you more, then figure out how many ounces you *desire* to have. Now calculate the total three amounts of money you want from the last question in ounces of gold.

5. Circle which Master Money Strategy you would like to use to generate wealth?

   a) M²S1 (Trading Time for Money)

   b) M²S2 (Trading Money for Money)

   c) M²S3 (Multiple Sources of Income)

Chapter 11

Futile Fear

"The only competition you will ever face is with your own ignorance."

-Bob Proctor

How many times a day do you fear something and then realize it was pointless? Fear controls the world. The majority of the population buy products or services based on fear. I used to live in fear because I was suffering from ignorance. This chapter demonstrates exactly how destructive FEAR is and how productive FAITH is. One of the natural laws of the universe is the Law of Polarity. This law states that every single thing in this universe has an opposite, for example, there is no hot without a cold, no top without a bottom, no front without a back, and no good without a bad. There are two sides to this law:

Knowledge **(ilm)** & Ignorance **(jahiliyyah)**

Ralph Waldo Trine once said, *"Nothing is good or bad, except our thinking makes it so."* Every thought you think is the start of an attitude, and attitude will make you or break you. YOU have the power to choose your thoughts. You can either choose to have negative or positive thoughts. That choice of thought turns into a feeling, and that feeling becomes a vibration. Vibration causes an action, which sets up an attraction to take place. This causes that initial thought, whether positive or negative, to manifest into physical form. Throughout all of history, religious scriptures have always confirmed this truth.

For example, in the Holy Quran, King Solomon commands his ministers to bring the Queen of Sheba's throne into his physical presence.

The Quran states in (27:30-40) that Solomon said: "Ye chiefs! Which of you can bring me her throne before they come to me in submission?"

Solomon's most knowledgeable genie said: "I will bring it to thee before thou rise from thy council: indeed, I have full strength for the purpose and may be trusted."

One who had knowledge of the book said: "I will bring it to thee within the wink of an eye!"

Then when Solomon saw the throne placed firmly before him, he said: "This is by the Grace of my Lord - to test me whether I am grateful or ungrateful and if any is grateful, truly his gratitude is a gain for his own soul; but if any is ungrateful, truly my Lord is Free of all Needs, Supreme in Honour!"

This lesson reinforces what Napoleon Hill and the boxing legend Muhammad Ali used to say: *Whatever my mind can conceive, and my heart can believe, I can achieve!*

Solomon's minister conceived the idea that he could use the Law of Attraction to manifest her throne in Solomon's presence within the blink of an eye. He believed that he had the power within his mind to accomplish this, based on the certainty of his knowledge and not blind faith. He thereby declared it with the assumption that he could, in fact, do it, and hence made his goal a physical reality. This was only possible because his *desire* was backed by 100% faith and 0% fear. This achievement is recognized and forever enshrined in these verses of the Holy Quran.

Did you know your Central Nervous System is the most complex electrical system in the world? I want you to IMAGINE for a second how many charges of energy are flying through your body which is activated by your brain cells just so you can write down your name with your hand. Another world of creation exists inside your body! When you think a *negative* thought for a second on a conscious level, before you know it, that *negative* thought makes its way to the subconscious level. The negative thought then turns into an idea, which sets up a vibration in your body known as **FEAR**. I have always been negatively affected by fear. I've transferred from school to school many times throughout my years of traditional education and no matter where I went, I would experience some form of bullying. It was either verbally or physically. My mother always told me to believe in the saying, *"sticks and stones may break my bones, but words will never hurt me!"*

Unfortunately, I did not believe that statement on a subconscious level, and that caused me to experience **FEAR**. It got to a point, where I used to have a fear of people, places, and random things. Every time I feared something, I would continue to put my focus towards that fear, and that attracted everything I didn't want into in my life. This led to negative experiences and eventually I faced depression. At the time, I had no clue what depression was, but now as I look back, I accept that I experienced a form of depression and it was all based on **FEAR**. The fear originated from either a past negative experience or a future frightening event. As a Sleepwalker, I did not know any better, and

I continued living in fear. I was mainly responsible for every negative thing that happened in the past because my fearful thinking was the *cause* and the *effect* was the negativity I attracted which put me into a low vibrational depressive state. The 'depression' only existed because I allowed it to with my mind. Below is a deeper explanation for you to understand my perspective on this subject.

According to the World Health Organization, in 2015, approximately 350 million humans worldwide suffered from depression. After reaching a state of *Conscious Awareness*, I have realized that **depression** is only created in the human mind. If you suffer from depression, understand that a cure for it exists. The cure can only take place if you are WILLING to put in the work to heal yourself by just doing one powerful thing. This requires you to take control of the golden gift you have which is your MIND. Let me explain how only one negative thought can create depression. In the book, *As A Man Thinketh*, James Allen said, ***"Fear has been known to kill a person faster than a speeding bullet."*** Did you know that FAITH and FEAR both demand that YOU believe in something that you **CANNOT** see? Fear is known to create destructive thoughts such as:

<u>we are not going to have enough money for that...</u>

<u>ahhh my life is ruined now!</u>

<u>things are getting from bad to worse!!!</u>

<u>I will never be able to pass this test...</u>

<u>how will I ever get married???</u>

Always remember fear is a very destructive vibration. If your mind is thinking of fearful thoughts, immediately a negative vibration grows in your body. This naturally causes your body to heat up with tension. Now this tensed energy needs to be expressed in some way, so it releases itself in the physical vibration of anxiety. This happens at warp speed that you don't even realize it! The feeling of anxiety is never *expressed*; it is almost always *suppressed*. Anxiety is a negative vibration that can only be suppressed and once the suppression takes place in your body, it then turns into **depression**. Depression slowly becomes a type of disease, which is a physical condition that puts your body, not at ease (dis-ease). If no healing is done to your mind, body, and soul, then your body reaches a low vibrational state of depression which eventually leads to disintegration. This is how you could end up deliberately destroying yourself by attracting things you don't want into your life all because of one fearful thought. All vibrations ultimately manifest, regardless of whether they are positive or negative. Based on my own perception, this is why depression is a self-inflicted state, and the root cause of this problem is not knowing how to control your thoughts. Throughout my years of being a Sleepwalker, it didn't even occur to me that I could change my emotional state by controlling any negative thoughts to eliminate fear. After I learned how to flip the switch from Tony Robbins, I was able to control my thoughts and feelings. If you use these three **M**aster Strategies, they will help you control your emotional state by avoiding constant negative thinking.

1) Mental State Shift

2) Physical State Shift

3) Fear Elimination Shift

I created a free virtual workshop that will show you how to use these 3 **M**aster Strategies. To gain access go to www.TheYoungMastermind.com/Fear

Make sure to download the workbook and print it out so you can do the activities while watching the videos.

"Worry is soul suicide."

- James Allen

How many times a day do you worry about something? I think you'd be shocked if you actually took out the time to count. Throughout my 18 years of being a sleepwalker, my mind experienced at least a billion thoughts of worry. This happened because I was living in ignorance; a lack of understanding. My burning desire for riches kept me motivated to strive for accomplishing specific goals no matter how impossible they seemed at the time. I set goals to generate residual income, speak on stages, purchase my first dream car, personally meet influential, powerful, and wealthy individuals. The moment I set those big goals, my reasoning faculty came in the way and got my mind to focus on all the potential problems that could arise. I allowed feelings of doubt and worry to control my thoughts which affected my body's vibration. These negative thoughts got my mind to imagine that the worst possible outcomes could actually manifest as this ignited the feeling of anxiety.

Thankfully, I changed my negative thoughts right before the state of depression could enter my mind. I was able to successfully transform my sleepwalker thoughts into mastermind thoughts because I realized that FEAR got me to believe in something I couldn't even see. It was at this moment in my life when I become consciously aware of the fact that I could choose to have FAITH instead of FEAR since it also required me to believe in the invisible. To conclude, all my big dreams that seemed impossible to achieve at one point because of all the false evidence appearing real, ended up shaping my reality in their own unique way at the perfect time!

"Change your thoughts, change your life"

- Wayne Dyer

Now you must be wondering how to avoid all of this stress and experience life without any pointless fear. It all starts with *belief*. If you have faith that is based on understanding, then you have the keys to freedom! KNOWLEDGE is the polar opposite of IGNORANCE. You cannot develop knowledge by accident, the only way to gain knowledge is by studying. *Studying* is the idea of investing in yourself and learning about who really you are and how much power you have locked up within you. The time you dedicate to study yourself will eventually bring you on the true path of light when your soul is ready for alignment. I choose to invest in myself by reading books that are full of wisdom, listening to audio recordings of successful people, purchasing courses, video programs and attending live seminars.

If you want to attract good things in life, you must make a firm decision that you actually want good things out of life. Below is a step by step process that you now have access to, so you can start making powerful decisions.

Step 1:

If you are enrolled in the **Master Decision Maker Program**, then you are aware of this statement. If you aren't then you can still use this statement every time you need to make an important decision:

"I AM committed to achieving this result and because I just stated that, I have naturally cut myself off from any other possibility other than achieving this desired outcome."

Step 2:

Start to hold the image of what you *desire* in your mind's eye. In order for the image of your desire to move onto the subconscious level, you must *feel* as if you already have it. You must have blind certainty and faith. Always remember **FAITH** and **FEAR** both demand you to believe in something invisible. So why fall on the path of **DARKNESS** and believe in fear like a sleepwalker? Just choose to do the opposite like a Mastermind and have faith by imagining all the good you want is already yours! If it is hard to believe at first, play a game with your mind and *act* as if you already possess the faith you need. This will automatically place you on the true path of **LIGHT**.

If you would like to learn the *4 Master Step Process* on how to make decisions like the world's most successful people do, then make a decision right now to invest in yourself because your mind is your most valuable asset.

Once you make the firm Master Decision that you will no longer live in the negative vibration of fear, then your mind will be able to *think* only positive thoughts. Instead of *worry*, you will *study* to gain an *understanding*, which will bring you to an inner realization of the lesson fear is trying to teach you. The positive vibration of your faith will diminish your fear and transmute your *anxiety* into *well-being*. All suppressed feelings of depression in your body will be transformed into your new state of *acceleration* as this positive feeling is expressed. Your heart will become tranquil, doubts will disappear, and your body will start to feel *at-ease* instead of always feeling *dis-ease*. Lastly, the destructive state of *disintegration* will remold itself into a productive state of *creation* and this will allow you to create your desired reality.

You can master this process by just allowing the positive energy to flow to and through you and then choose to think with **FAITH** and not with **FEAR**. Remember, the choice is ultimately yours, either be a Sleepwalker and live with **IGNORANCE** or be Mastermind and live with **KNOWLEDGE**.

At this stage, I desired to only stay in the vibrational frequency of a Mastermind so I had to study in order to develop an understanding. The next chapter is where I found what I was looking for all along... MY PURPOSE.

Master Action Plan

1. What does the Law of Polarity mean to you?

2. Do you want to be the Master of FEAR or do you want to be the Master of FAITH ?

Explain why:

3. At the end of this chapter, I provided you with a powerful statement from one of my Master Programs for FREE! It allows you to make a successful decision whenever you need to.

It's called the *'Master Decision Maker'*, write that statement below. If you can't remember it, then you should re-read this chapter at least one more time.

4. In this chapter you became aware of the secret to eliminating a form of 'depression' from your life.

In your own words, explain how this process takes place starting from one negative thought.

Chapter 12

Master the Present

"Realize deeply that the present moment is all you have. Make NOW the primary focus of your life."

-Eckhart Tolle

When is the last time you actually listened to that inner voice from within and followed what it suggested? Remember that feeling of regret when you knew you should have listened to that inner voice? That voice was your heart speaking to you. The subconscious is the emotional part of your personality, in other words, it's like your heart. Religious scriptures confirm this truth. King Solomon once said, *"As a person thinketh in their heart, so are they."* The early Greeks were aware of the fact that the subconscious and the heart are one. When you are sleeping your subconscious mind is awake and your heart continues to pump itself without any conscious effort because your subconscious is in control. Your beautiful heart and your powerful subconscious mind both work in harmony and speak to and through you. If you listen to that inner voice, you will always be successful in everything you do. There were hundreds of times in my life when I ignored that voice from within that knew the truth. Whenever I would be in the middle of making a serious decision, I would consciously be aware of that voice that was telling me what to do but I would choose to do the opposite, even though deep down I knew that would be the wrong thing to do. I didn't listen to my inner voice because I was ignorant. Eventually, I would regret not listening to my heart; the subconscious. Once I started to develop *Conscious Awareness*, I was able to tune into the voice from within and pay attention to the inner truth with pure focus. After I started listening to my inner voice, I would act upon the suggestion, and never regret any of my decisions. The only way you will be able to hear the voice from within is when you are grateful for the present moment. Realize that every moment is a gift from the universe to you regardless if you think the moment is negative or positive. In every present moment of your life, you are receiving gifts. It's called 'the *present*' for a reason. Another word for **'Gift'** is **'Present.'** Once you breathe in deeply and accept the gift you are receiving in every moment, you'll come to the realization that you have an ABUNDANCE of air to breathe from which is keeping you alive every moment. If you want to always be happy, just *feel* grateful for your powerful heart that beats without your conscious attention. That is the present you receive every second without doing anything in return.

Did you know that all the great leaders from history disagreed on several things, but they all agreed on one idea? They all understood the truth to this, *'We become what we think about.'* Understand that thoughts become things. Quantum physics tells us that thought is energy because thought waves are cosmic waves that penetrate over the scope of time and space. No energy is more powerful than thought *energy*. You must realize that you are a creative being with infinite resources. You have been given the ability to THINK a thought and form an idea. This is the highest function you as a human being are capable of doing as the highest form of creation. Your thoughts can become things ONLY when you focus on them, regardless if you have positive or negative thoughts. The problem is, like billions of other humans, you were most likely programmed to imagine the negative outcome in your mind before it physically happened, and before you know it, that negative outcome you imagined ends up becoming an actual reality. This is because when you focus on what you don't want, that's exactly what you end up attracting into your life. The key is to figure out exactly what you DON'T want, so you can direct your thought *energy* to focus on what you DO want. Tony Robbins once told me, *"Where focus goes, energy flows."* If only you knew how powerful your thoughts were, you would NEVER dare even to think a single negative thought ever again!

Everything in life starts with a simple thought that leads to an idea, and by writing down the idea, a plan of action is created. Every single building in the world began with a thought. Once the landlord accepted the thought, he started to believe in the idea of developing the land into an actual property. This owner then took this thought to the ministry and applied for permits after consulting with an architect. The architect used the creativity that every human being has to visualize and draw out a sketch of the building's exterior and interior. After that, a scaled model of the building was made for the architect. Then the construction crew was hired, money was raised, the ground was broken, and construction started. Eventually, the building appeared, people began living in it, unique memories were created, but remember this whole thing all began with a single *thought*. Nothing has or ever will be created without thought *energy*. Masterminds use their thoughts to create what they ***desire***. Sleepwalkers use their thoughts to create what they don't want.

This very moment should be a blessed moment for you because I believe, the information in this book expanded your level of awareness in whichever way. If you already haven't realized that, then, realize it NOW by *feeling* grateful that YOU can use your own eyes to read these words, and as your brain processes this information, your mind understands what you are reading at the exact same time. This shouldn't shock you because you are the highest form of creation who has the power and ability to originate a thought at any moment in time. This is being aware and *Mastering the Present*. My purpose for writing this book was to expand your level of awareness, so you can eventually reach the ideal state of *Conscious Awareness* and become a MasterMind!

Mr. Leland Van De Wall shared the seven levels of awareness with Bob Proctor. Bob shared them with *The Young Mastermind*, and now I AM sharing them with YOU.

The Seven Levels of Awareness:

7) **Mastery:** *Respond...Think and Plan*

6) **Experience:** *Your Actions Change Your RESULTS*

5) **Discipline:** *Give Yourself a Command and then Follow it*

4) **Individual:** *You Express Your Uniqueness*

3) **Aspiration:** *You Desire Something Greater in Life*

2) **Mass:** *Follow the Masses...your old programming*

1) **Animal:** *Re-act...Fight or Flight*

Did you know there are layers of virus code that block your level of awareness from expanding? These virus codes were planted into the garden of your mind from the moment you were born. They restrict you from living your dream life. The goal is to raise your awareness to the level of **Mastery**. Understand, the result you are getting in life are a direct reflection of how aware your mind is. The only way you can improve every part of your life is by expanding your awareness. If you expand your level of awareness, then you need to set goals that make you stretch. The purpose of a goal is to grow. The only way you can experience growth is when you go after a goal that you really really want. It's your heart's desire. Always remember that you don't need to worry about 'HOW' your goal will manifest. It is NOT your business to worry about how exactly the process will work.

The Wright brothers, never knew how they were going to get the plane off the ground. They just knew it was going to happen. They used their faculty of imagination to see the plane life of the ground before it physically happened. If you study the lives of the world's most successful humans on this planet who create phenomenal things that serve humanity, they never are able to explain the "HOW' in exact detail. They know that what they desire is bound to happen regardless of any conditions, circumstances or environments so they just do it. These humans are able to achieve their extraordinary goals becuase they constantly increase their level of awareness. Bob Proctor taught me that, effective goals inspire people to reach very high levels of awareness. Make sure you never set a goal that you already know how to get or a goal you think you can probably get. Only set goals that excite and scare you at the exact same time, because those are the type of goals that will allow you to grow.

THINK of someone you know who lives a life that you admire or dream of living. That person that you just thought of is only able to live in that particular way because they are aware of how to. If you were aware, then you could as well. Each and every single thing you desire to have can be yours within the wink of an eye but only if you become aware. When you expand your awareness to such a deep level, you will be able to live the dream life you have always dreamt of, have everything you have always desired, and be the person you've always envisioned yourself to become. A complete happy, healthy and wealthy life is all a result of higher levels of awareness. To increase awareness, you must concentrate your thought *energy* on studying superior knowledge and ancient wisdom. The most efficient and effective way to learn from a mentor is by investing in their coaching programs, mentorship services and attending their live seminars. Keep in mind, the money you invest will always be worth the investment because their products and services are all designed to help you grow to such an extent that your future progeny would benefit from the knowledge and wisdom you gain. At a young age, I have invested more than $50,000 to expand my level of awareness, but the information I have learned is worth trillions! This is the only way to eliminate the layers of virus code. This is how the world's most successful people did it and this is how you are going to do it as well if you want your mind's level of awareness to expand.

Bob Proctor once wrote, "The only competition you will ever face is with your own ignorance." If you don't want to be a **Sleepwalker** who lives in ignorance, but you want to be a **Mastermind**, then be open-minded and learn to accept new information, even though it may not initially make sense to you. Be willing to give every single opportunity a chance in life before closing your doors. Once you recognize an opportunity, make the *quantum leap* into a new environment. If you want to grow in life, you must be ready to escape your comfort zone. If you are satisfied with your current results and you feel safe, this state is very dangerous in the long run. Let me explain why. **Sleepwalkers** set goals which they know how to get, eventually, they achieve their goals and become satisfied, which causes them to *plateau*. On the other hand, **Masterminds** set goals that they don't know 'HOW' to get. Once they achieve their goals and *feel* grateful, they become dissatisfied with their current results in life, as this builds a ***desire*** to accomplish even higher goals which cause them to ***grow***.

There is a basic Law of Life which states that each and every single thing in this universe is either in a state of Creation or Disintegration. That means that if YOU are not growing, you are dying. If you are not creating, you are sleeping. Strive to improve any area of your life in some way or the other. Just do small things in a great way, every single day, but focus on doing things that will take you to your desired destination in life! If you really want to dominate your path in life; succeed in every endeavor; and improve your life intellectually, emotionally, spiritually, physically, socially, and financially, then you should apply everything that was shared throughout this book. I would be very honored and grateful if the *Mastermind Seminars, Universal Masterminding, or Mastermind Mentorship*, left a genuine positive impact on your life.

*"Instead of saying, **'we want this, and we want that'** - just do it."*

-Ameerah Al-Taweel

The most important part of
mastering the present is
acknowledging and accepting
the *feelings*,
thoughts, and
bodily sensations
you have in this very moment.

take a Minute and listen to
Your bodY…

Do This Now

Inspiration to find your Purpose

"There is a plan and a purpose, a value to every life, no matter what its location, age, gender or disability."
— **Sharron Angle**

"The two most important days in your life are the day you are born and the day you find out why."
— **Mark Twain**

"Self-transformation commences with a period of self-questioning. Questions lead to more questions, bewilderment leads to new discoveries, and growing personal awareness leads to transformation in how a person lives. Purposeful modification of the self only commences with revising our mind's internal functions. Revamped internal functions eventually alter how we view our external environment."
— **Kilroy J. Oldster**

"...and when you want something, all the universe conspires in helping you to achieve it."
— **Paulo Coelho**

"Success without fulfillment is the ultimate failure in life."
— **Tony Robbins**

Master the Present

*"Reality is merely an illusion, albeit
a very persistent one"*

-Albert Einstein

Young Masterminds see the invisible, believe in the incredible, and receive what the masses call... 'Impossible'!

*"In my world, **'reality'** is negotiable,
success is inevitable, and
my vision is attainable."*

-Young Mastermind

Do you want to be a

Young Mastermind

or

Do you want to be a

Sleepwalker?

THE CHOICE IS YOURS.

To access your FREE

Master Manifestation Method Video Program

Go to: www.TheYoungMastermind.com/MMM

Follow the journey with Muhammad Ali on social media:

Instagram.com/Young.Mastermind

YouTube.com/YoungMastermind

Facebook.com/MasterAlimind

Twitter.com/MasterAlimind

Learn more about Young Masterminds Institute of Success by understanding our products and services at:

TheYoungMastermind.com

Acknowledgements

I would like to thank YOU for being you and for taking out your most limited asset; TIME, to read my book. As you know, I AM on the mission to show **1 BILLION** human beings how to become the Masters of their own Minds, and this mission starts with YOU. I need your help to impact billions. I would be so happy and forever GRATEFUL if you could do 1 simple thing for me. Post a picture of this book or a quick video about your experience after reading *The Young Mastermind*. It doesn't matter whether you have 100 or 1,000000 human beings who follow/subscribe to you on social media. What matters is that people follow YOU for a reason, and you have the power to help anyone improve their own life. You wouldn't need to do anything other than just share this book becuase remember if even one of your followers reads this book, they would learn how to transform from being a Sleepwalker into a Mastermind. If you genuinely "love" your fans, this is a cool way to show them how grateful you are for their support. So please share this direct link: **TheYoungMastermind.com/freebook** with your followers, so they can easily get this ebook version of *The Young Mastermind* for FREE. Keep in mind, I humbly requested you to do this, not to serve our egos and make money together, but so we can serve more people and spread positive vibes together!

I want you to understand at this very moment that all of the superior knowledge and ancient wisdom that is shared at the Young Masterminds Institute of Success will is priceless. At the end of the day, I have dedicated my entire life to serving billions of humans in this universe including YOU, so this connection you may feel is just the beginning of our mastermind relationship! Hey, look forward to my new books, documentaries, online master classes and live seminars in a city near you!

www.ingramcontent.com/pod-product-compliance
Lightning Source LLC
Chambersburg PA
CBHW071829080526
44589CB00012B/963